# A
# CANARY
# INVESTIGATES

**DIABOLICAL HEALTH EFFECTS FROM WIRELESS TECHNOLOGY,
CRIMES AGAINST HUMANITY,
AND STRATEGIES TO SURVIVE THE 21ST CENTURY**

CHERY LANNE

ISBN: 979-8-89694-517-8 - eBook
ISBN: 979-8-89694-518-5 - Paperback

Cartoons provided by Quickcartoons, graphics and images provided by 123RF royalty free images, and photos provided by Chery Lanne unless stated otherwise. Cover image is Chery Lanne walking down a country road in Wheeling, Illinois, USA in 2014.

# PRAISE FOR CHERY LANNE

- to have the courage to tell it like it is

"This book is brilliant! It outlines all the major issues we all face every day and provides practical hands–on solutions for how to heal, how to improve your health, and how to increase your energy levels. It lays out very specifically what we are dealing with every day of our lives; and is a "Wake–up Call" for many who may not be aware of what we are being exposed to. This book provides detailed information about what is really happening in our world and provides practical solutions. How did they con everyone into leaving their Wi-Fi, Bluetooth and mobile phones on 24/7? Why would you not turn these devices OFF when not using them and when you sleep? Especially as your brain reads it as light which stops your melatonin production — not only affecting your sleep — but suppressing free–radical production required to clean up cancer cells in your body? Did you know that turning OFF your Wi-Fi when not in use will save you around $1,500+ a year on your electricity bill. How hard do you have to work for that?"

Karen Winter Dip.HSc.Kin.
Advanced Specialist Kinesiology Practitioner & Angelic Universal Regression Alchemist

**A Canary Investigates**, is a vital read for anyone concerned about the hidden dangers of modern technology. Chery Lanne successfully combines hands-on research & testing with practical advice, offering a powerful warning about the unspoken health risks of EMF exposure. This book takes a deep dive into the political and corporate landscape surrounding 5G and EMF regulation, highlighting how corporate interests have outweighed public health concerns. As a building biologist experiencing first hand EMF and 5G poisoning, the author is well positioned to verify what many have rightfully questioned, and now this brave canary is sounding the alarm for all to hear."

M. Aves. Architect

"I thoroughly enjoyed this book. Everyone who cares about their health and their family's health and well-being needs to read **A Canary Investigates**. It's such an eye opener to what is happening all around us, and that people don't do anything about it. Excellent read."

Jenny Smith. Mould Consultancy

**DISCLAIMER:** My experience is my personal experience, as I see it, and what other people see may be in conflict with what I see, but that doesn't negate the facts. I am not medically trained, I do not diagnose, treat or offer a cure for ailments. I am an environmental health professional, trained to diagnose an environment to detect pathogens, toxins and non-native energy fields known to cause biological harm; and trained to prescribe a solution. Becoming sensitive to radio frequencies and electromagnetic fields enabled me to use my skills, to save my life. No one else has offered to do that. Contact a professional Building Biologist or trained EMF Testing Technician to assess all electromagnetic force (EMF) and electromagnetic radiation (EMR). To be safe, question their integrity and use your discernment. This book is for education purposes, to identify the invisible enemy people can't see, and learn what to do about it. What you do with this information is totally up to you.

**SMART
CANARY**

**Escaping the wireless world could be the smartest
move ever invented. You're about to find out why.**

From aware to awake takes time – the faster you wake up the better!

Some names have been changed for privacy, and to protect the innocent.

# DEDICATION

This book is dedicated to Maria (dec), Arthur
Firstenberg (dec) and EMF Canaries worldwide.

Without canaries exposing biological effects from wireless radiation,
we are none the wiser and in a very precarious position.

When you don't know what you don't know, you can't pack your own
parachute (lifesaving system). Until someone warns you, you have no
idea what's harming you.   Once you know, you can take precautionary
action and rise above the deception and trickery of Profits @ Any Cost.

*"The things you do for yourself are gone when you are gone,*

*but the things you do for others remain as your legacy."*

Anonymous

# CONTENTS

# INTRODUCTION
# Author's Insights and Inspiration
## By Chery Lanne

A CANARY INVESTIGATES is a drop in the ocean of the Great Awakening. At the time of writing, the world is waking up, but for me and others in the know, not fast enough. Hopefully, one day we will know the whole truth, but in the meantime, trust your gut feelings and listen to your innate intelligence, not the main stream news.

This book is my story and my investigations into crimes against humanity. It's taken me years to uncover hidden knowledge and learn the truth about medicine, cancer, healing and rejuvenation. I discovered the jewel in the crown of knowledge when I studied Building Biology. It revealed the truth about man-made energy, including wireless frequencies from new technology, and how they play a diabolical role in disease manifestation. When I studied Building Biology, to learn how to create healthy homes, I had no idea I'd become an Electromagnetic Radiation Specialist (EMRS). And never in my wildest dreams did I think the cumulative effect of **electromagnetic radiation (EMR),** from mobile (cell) phones, phone towers, and dirty electricity would nearly kill me. No way did I expect I'd be the evidence of crimes against humanity, affecting millions of people around the world.

Prior to 2020 I was focused on helping people detect a variety of biological toxins causing havoc with their health. Providing solutions was part of the job, so when I started to have increasingly bizarre symptoms, I did some testing and identified immediately what the problem was, and set about fixing it. **I knew doctors could not help me**. That fact alone is reason to learn more about EMF and wireless technology, because not knowing could be the greatest risk to life this century. Back in 2017, when I started to have mild health effects from EMR, the last thing I expected was that it would transition into symptoms of multiple sclerosis, chronic fatigue and total physical dysfunction by 2021. I was not aware at that time that there were millions of canaries having the same diabolical effects from technology as I was.

In days gone by canaries alerted miners of imminent danger and the need to get out of the coal mine, or perish from inhaling toxic gas. Coal miners used canaries as life-savers. Canaries these days are electrically hypersensitive (EHS) people like me, often ignored, mistreated by doctors or treated as inconvenient friends when they ask people to turn off their phones because they feel the negative effects. Those unable to live with increased radiofrequency radiation, have literally been ringing alarm bells around the world, warning people of this EHS humanitarian emergency. However, instead of being heralded as life-savers, they are ostracised, and even ridiculed by those that have no idea modern technology is dangerous.

Before I became a canary my attention was on cancer due to a history of death by cancer in my family. I decided years ago it would be beneficial to know as much about cancer prevention as possible. Little did I know EMF and cancer are connected. What I discovered after years of research, was that the medical profession is no closer to preventing cancer than they were 60 years ago. This developed into a passion project when I discovered cancer is a money-making venture, fuelled by corruption and collusion worldwide. This was not what I expected at all, and for that reason I realised sharing my knowledge and what I learned from studying Building Biology and ultimately Electrobiology could be life-changing on a grand scale. My experiences, documented in this book, are evidence we need a better education.

In my opinion, the biggest cover-up in the world today is the manufacture of disease. I am not alone; many experts share the same belief. I'm taking on a massive task, as are other canaries, good doctors and scientists, warning the world of the danger to all life on Earth. Humanity may not survive this onslaught of man-made frequencies if the lack of truth, lack of transparency and lack of good will in elite circles is not exposed, and rectified.

Building Biology includes many subjects, one of which is mould training. A mould spore is similar in size to a virus (about 3-4 microns; a micron is a millionth of a metre). Mould spores and viruses are not stopped by a face mask. You would need a P3 respirator to filter particles that size. When I investigated further, I realised nothing about the COVID outbreak made sense. Mask wearing, distancing and what the World Health Organisation, governments, and the (so-called) medical experts worldwide introduced to stop the spread was not science backed. It was as if they had lost every ounce of common sense, and it appeared as if they were inventing tactics and mandates out of thin air.

It's vitally important you're aware of the truth, to enable you to deal with an agenda put in place by people and organisations worldwide, which seems to be designed to inflict great harm. But first a little about me and why I didn't fall for bogus protocols. Instead, I realised there is an even greater and more sinister agenda at play.

## Cancer Left a Lasting Legacy; a Quest to Find the Truth

My life-long inspiration to seek truth about cancer came from being told by a neighbour, I was the reason my mother died of cancer at 45. It wasn't true, but I suspect that belief was formed because my mum became sick after I was born. Cancer wasn't diagnosed immediately, but when it was, it was too late to do anything.

The photo below is me at my mother's funeral in 1960. She died of cancer before I was two years old.

Losing my mother was not my most earthshattering moment in life, I was too young to remember; it was my farther dying when I was sixteen years old. He had been my mentor and brains-trust, teaching me many things. If not for him I would not be the person I am today. Most importantly my dad taught me how to use my common sense; to always do the right thing; and never be idle at work because they don't pay you for doing nothing. Three things I've never forgotten.

In 1978 I met the love of my life, a carpenter like my dad, who had lost his father in a workplace accident when he was eight years old. We had an appreciation of life and how precious it is from a young age. We married within months of meeting, and built a life and a business together in the building and construction industry. Hard work and investing in property paid off and we were able to purchase our dream farm, a 163-acre cropping and grazing property in 1995, where we raised our four boys.

## Life Was Good Until It Wasn't

Our business life came to a crashing halt in 2012, due to an economic downturn in the construction industry in our home state of Tasmania, an idyllic island, south of the mainland of Australia. Capital works funding was drastically reduced by state and federal governments, which caused massive layoffs in the construction industry, resulting in insufficient commercial projects to keep our business alive. Fallout from the 2008 global financial crisis was still having an effect, which meant money was scarce. We decided to move to Queensland, a northern state of Australia, along with many others in search of work.

Prior to 2012, a Chamber of Commerce and Industry business assessment complemented us for meeting and managing business requirements, including safety and quality management systems that met international standards. The assessment identified marketing and communications as our weakest skillset. After being in business for thirty-three years I thought I needed to go to university to study marketing and communication, only to find I would be trained to work for Telstra, a telecommunications company. Instead, I googled; *how to be successful* and, *how to live to 100, and not get cancer.*

A world of alternative education opened up to me. I studied with Brian Tracy, Eben Pagan and Rich Dad Coaching; a coaching business for entrepreneurs, founded by Robert Kiyosaki, author of Rich Dad, Poor Dad, in the USA.

An alternate education changed my perception and beliefs about business and how people survived and thrived doing the things they loved. We travelled around the world in 2014, enjoying cultural experiences in Dubai, London, and New York, and ended our adventure at a marketing summit, in Chicago. A bonus for undertaking Accelerate High Growth Business Training, provided by Eben Pagan. It was brilliant, and that's where Alfred Pacheco gave me his book **EMF Health Alert; *The #1 Guide for Reducing Electromagnetic Pollution in Your Home***. Electromagnetic pollution wasn't on my radar. Although, after reading his book, I did chuck out our microwave oven and switched from a wireless keyboard and mouse to a wired keyboard and wired mouse. I wasn't really aware of the risks to health from electro-pollution, because no one in the medical or health arena had ever mentioned it. Later on, I realised 2014 was the beginning of a great awakening, on multiple levels.

I thought I'd solved my - *what do I need to know about business* question, but not - *what do I need to know about cancer prevention.* Cancer still puzzled me, until Nicole Bijlsma, (founder of the College of Environmental Studies in Victoria), gave a talk about sick buildings, environmental toxins, and the science and art of Building Biology at a Wellness Summit in Melbourne, Australia. I contacted Nicole in 2015 and she convinced me to study Building Biology, if my intention was to help people create healthy homes. At the time I believed it was talcum powder that caused my mother's cancer. I was partly correct, but not totally aware of toxic environmental exposures, and how a multitude of cancer-causing agents are found in homes and workplaces worldwide.

During my training, it felt like I'd hit the jackpot; this education opened my eyes to the hidden causes of autoimmune disorders, Alzheimer's, ADD, ADHD, autism, cancer, and chronic inflammatory response syndrome (CIRS) a condition totally new to me. CIRS is caused by mould in water-damaged buildings (WDB). I realised the building industry is vastly unaware of CIRS and why preventing water damage and condensation in a building is a critical design requirement, that needs to be considered at every stage of planning and development.

My passion was and still is prevention of cancer and disease, and my aim was to help people create a home that sustains and nurtures a healthy life. In Australia, Building Biologists, under Nicole's guidance, are classified as environmental health practitioners, trained to diagnose environments, mostly homes, to detect environmental and biological toxins scientifically proven to cause negative health effects, which often go undiagnosed or misdiagnosed by doctors. I had no inkling my training would literally be a life saver.

**Building Biology, is a science for our time.** Not many people know the science of Building Biology exists, which is a crying shame, because it's the most brilliant and beneficial science illuminating the truth about environmental exposures. Building Biologists identify many causes of illness and disease originating from the built environment, and specify solutions to make homes and workplaces safer and healthier to support natural healing.

The world is playing Russian roulette with the increase of wireless frequencies, and rarely do people comprehend the capacity for invisible waves in the air to cause devastating health effects. My aim is to make you smarter than your smart phone, because building your brain power is the best defence against a monster you can't see, or detect without specialised equipment. You can't feel frequencies unless you've gained conscious awareness, or a sixth sense like canaries, and you can't detect them unless you have an EMF meter or radio frequency (RF) analyser to identify where this un-natural energy is coming from. Wireless technology is not the only bullet in the gun. By reading this book you'll learn how to become an environmental detective and how to unload the gun. In a nutshell, this book exposes the truth mainstream education does not.

Beware! Believing the truth will set you free is a misnomer; the truth will make you very angry. Once you know the truth, you can form your own opinion and decide if the rollout of more wireless devices, without prior warning of the dangers, could be labelled a crime against humanity.

Co-ordinated and controlling multinational companies, I call Profits @ Any Cost, dominate the media and systems of governance we follow in blind faith. I discovered the hard way that Profits @ Any Cost can't be trusted. In days gone by I was totally spellbound by the systems of control I believed had our best interests at heart. Those beliefs have been shattered and replaced with an understanding of how we've been tricked into believing global governments, and international non-government organisations (NGOs) care about humanity. What I know for sure is without the information in this book you cannot protect yourself, or your family, from an invisible, invasive energy, classified as a Class 2B Carcinogen (cancer causing agent) by the International Agency for Research on Cancer

(IARC). It's impossible to comprehend the damage being done and no one in power seems to care about the devastation it causes.

When the telecommunications companies, with support from governments, rolled out third, fourth and fifth generation technology (3G, 4G & 5G), it increased wireless radiation in the built environment to alarming levels, causing many people to react negatively to this unnatural energy. When the same mechanisms of control announced the Covid-19 pandemic worldwide, I had no idea what we were in for. Events of 2020 opened my eyes to a world of corruption and a world waking up, like never before.

There's a positive side to learning the truth, and what the remedies are, from a physical and mental perspective. It turns you into an enlightened, conscious and competent individual, able to harness innate intelligence and embrace natural wisdom. If the Profits @ Any Cost, multinational companies, could bottle it they'd put a patent on it to remain in control. Luckily, they can't patent nature, or innate intelligence; the two things we have in abundance. Learning how to master your God given gifts is worth more than money can buy. In a nutshell this book exposes, enlightens, and empowers you to be in control. It provides information to enable you to take responsibility for the results you get. I expose how everyone has been misled and identify what's needed to survive. You'll learn:

- Why an alternate education is life-saving.
- Why conscious competence helps regain control of your life.
- Why canaries are a sign of crimes against humanity.
- How a multitude of health effects are caused by wireless radiation.
- How "Profits @ Any Cost" companies and agencies get away with murder.
- How coordinated and controlling multinational companies and government agencies dominate the systems of governance we follow in blind faith.

- How 5ᵗʰ Generation technology (5G) is designed to monitor and control you, without your consent. It's SMART for the wrong reason.

**Best Takeaways:**

- What to do to reduce wireless radiation exposure, to reduce or prevent biological harm.
- What the longest-lived people in the world do, that most don't.
- Why saving your children's future potential, could save humanity.
- How the science of Building Biology is used to sustain health and/ or regain health.
- How to heal with Nature's help - mostly for free.
- The ultimate takeaway is the understanding of how the world has been controlled for a long time, without our consent.

If this is your first introduction to the Great Awakening, don't keep it to yourself because profiteering from ignorance has been going on for a long, long time. My aim is to empower you to take charge of the results you get, and maybe some of you may want to help create a better world.

**A bit of clarification before we dive in.** In Australia we use the term; mobile phone for cell phone; telephone tower for cell phone tower or radio mast, and the metric system (metres, millimetres and kilometres), not the imperial system (feet, inches and miles). Spelling is based on where the information came from. Please make allowances for variation in grammar and context based on original quotes from various experts in countries around the world.

**If you are not familiar with Building Biology**, or how wireless technology sits inside the electromagnetic spectrum, don't panic. I'll explain things along the way. Learning happens in stages, and if you're unclear about frequencies at first, keep reading, it will make sense in the end. Learning what 5G is may seem pointless, but it's no different to learning to drive a car, or learning how to operate a computer. It's a necessity in our modern world and you'll get there in the end.

Because terms for man-made electrical frequencies can be confusing, I'll paint a little picture to help you get your head around it. Take an imaginary X-ray of electrical wires in your walls. All the wires have an electromagnetic field (EMF). EMF is really an electromagnetic force pushing energy along the wires. EMF can be detected in the air emanating outwards from electrical circuits, electrical appliances and technology. Often you can hear a hum near transformers on the street as the voltage (the force) is reduced from high voltage wires, typically from 7,200 volts down to 240 volts, to power household appliances. Sometimes the term electromagnetic radiation (EMR) is used for EMF but in this book EMR refers specifically to invisible electromagnetic force travelling through the air, and it's often referred to as radio frequency radiation (RFR), or just radio frequencies (RF). This form of energy is used to transmit data on an electrical charged light wave. Think of an RF wave as an invisible clothesline with packets of information pegged to it. Information is being transmitted from a source, like a telephone transmission tower connected to a source of information on the internet, and radiated to a mobile phone or to a Wi-Fi modem that's configured to talk to your computer or tablet/iPad.

Other terms for EMR/RFR include: wireless radiation, microwave radiation, microwaves, Wi-Fi, Bluetooth, and Hotspot. In some instances, EMF will include electric fields, magnetic fields, electromagnetic energy (EME) and dirty electricity (DE), or dirty power, technically referred to as electromagnetic interference (EMI). Sometimes in this book EMF covers all electromagnetic frequencies, unless otherwise stated.

"Holy heck!" I hear you say. This is mind boggling, but don't let it bother you because I've included a **Glossary** at the end of the book, and a graphic to help explain what the electromagnetic spectrum is and how the radio frequency spectrum sits inside the electromagnetic spectrum. We all live with this energy in our environment, every day of our life. Hang in there, even if you don't understand at first; the lessons learned in this book, could be life-saving for you and your family. For investigators, technical geniuses in the making or for those more curious than most, I provide links to research, websites and books, should you wish to increase your competence. Even if you're only a little bit curious, learning more could be life-changing. Refer to the **Endnotes: Being inquisitive and questioning everything changes what you believe to be true.**

This book is designed to save your life, or help you get more life out of life. It is a serious subject, but hopefully the stories and the solutions provide a way to bridge the gap between unconscious incompetence and conscious competence ie. the level of learning you need to survive in this wireless world. In the end I hope you enjoy your new found wisdom, and apply it willingly.

*"Truth resides on the road less travelled, and it's well worth exploring, for life's sake" ~ Chery Lanne*

# FOREWORD
## by Dr Priyanka Bandara

C anaries, the little yellow birds, were used by miners from the 1800s - 1980s to detect noxious gases such as carbon monoxide in mines, because they were more sensitive to these gases than humans. Their distress or death alerted miners to evacuate or take protective actions. The term 'canary in the coal mine' now serves as a metaphor for environmental warning signals. Like the miners who observed the harm to the canaries and took precautions, we are meant to be using our intelligence to observe and study the world around us in order to protect ourselves and our families.

### Are we enabled observers anymore?

As a seasoned medical researcher and educator, it is with a heavy heart that I have to say "No we are not! On the contrary, we are flying blind!!!" Let me explain a little in this forward. **A Canary Investigates** is a book I urge you to read every page of, and heed the knowledge it imparts, especially if you are serious about protecting your health and your loved ones. Protecting your health in the 2020s is a completely different game, even to the recent past. You can no longer entirely rely on the mainstream advice from health professionals, and you will see why when you read this book. Although I have known Chery Lanne for several years, this book convinced me that she is not only a conscious canary, but also a caring, compassionate, conscientious, competent and courageous one. This is her gift to you, the reader. May I ask you to sit under a tree on a sunny day, read, ponder and make a pledge to protect yourself and your loves ones. Stand up for your right to life as a sovereign human being – with a healthy mind, body & spirit.

Around the year 2015, I realised that a particular 'future projection graph' shown at a medical conference I attended at the turn of this century, which at the time I perceived as an erroneous piece of work on the part of the presenter – the pharmaceutical industry – might prove to be correct. **The prediction, was that psychotropic medicines would have the highest growth leading to 2020** (not highest sales but rapidly escalating growth from quite low levels).

Psychotropic medicines are the chemical treatments for mental health problems: anxiety – depression – schizophrenia - bipolar disorder - sleep disorders etc., arising out of disruption to the production/action of natural chemicals in our bodies called neurotransmitters: serotonin, dopamine, gamma-aminobutyric acid (GABA), norepinephrine etc. The mental health burden in our human society in the 21$^{st}$ century has been expanding, even affecting children which is grossly abnormal, and it truly breaks my heart! There had been a significant increase in presentation of mental health problems and prescription of psychotropic agents in children and adolescents in the 1990s, with a reported 'sharp' increase from 1999. You have to wonder why?

On the surface of the broader medical field, it didn't look like we were heading for a mental health crisis back in the year 2000. However, Big Pharma knew! To us, academic medical researchers, the big problems seemed to be the increasing burden of chronic physical diseases that were the biggest killers - cardiovascular disease, cancer, diabetes and other conditions in the metabolic disease basket. Back then, I was a co-investigator and project manager of a large National Institute of Health (NIH), USA - funded study into liver disease at the Royal Prince Alfred and Westmead hospitals (as an academic of the School of Medicine, at the University of

Sydney). Committed and conscientious, I was confident that we (the Western health system) were making good progress in understanding how diseases developed at cellular and molecular levels (pathophysiology) and we would reduce human suffering and increase quality of life, in the coming decades.

By the end of 2012, I realised how bright-eyed and naïve I had been. **There has been no genuine interest in our medical system in identifying the real causes of chronic diseases and preventing them or resolving them.** Instead, the focus is disease 'management' with pharmaceutical, surgical and other therapeutic intervention. There is a monstrously greedy industry behind the sophisticated and clinically clean façade of modern healthcare, and when we are busy serving that interface, we are oblivious to the back end of it. Some (perhaps most) purposely avoid looking at the dangerous and unethical side even when pointed to it. After the long break I took to be a stay-at-home mother for my children, particularly a sick son (who thankfully recovered and thrived once the root causes of his sickness were removed), I was able to see a much bigger picture, (but still not fully). I decided to dedicate my expertise, time and effort to correct at least a few wrongs in the public health field.

By 2015, after spending four years intensely studying the published research on the health impacts of man-made electromagnetic radiation (EMR) exposure, the most common form being radiofrequency (RF) EMR emanating from our favourite wireless gadgets, I was deeply concerned. The collective evidence converging from the vast body of scientific studies (human studies and laboratory animal or cell culture studies) that I scrutinised, indicated that 'wireless radiation' could be the biggest culprit that destroys health of humanity and other forms of life - in stealth mode - in the 21$^{st}$ century – the fantastic digital age!

Due to the rapidly increasing 'deployment' (a military term) of wireless communications and surveillance technologies, the microwave (MW) part of the RF-EMR spectrum (frequency from 300 MHz to 300 GHz), an entirely unnatural exposure to life on earth, has been increasing in our environment by leaps and bounds. The scientific evidence indicated that it is not only a potent cause of mental health problems, but also a cause of serious physical diseases – cancer, cardiovascular disease, neurodegenerative diseases, immune diseases, metabolic and hormonal diseases.

Declassified American military documents revealed that the military medical researchers and the World Health Organization (WHO) had conducted thorough research and knew by the 1970s that microwave radiation (RF-EMR), initially used for radar, caused cancer, cardiovascular disease and a whole host of diseases. As a matter of fact, this invisible artificial agent can cause or exacerbate all ills because it penetrates all our body tissue and disrupts, damages and eventually destroys cells. This happens at the base of the multi-step processes of chronic disease development.

**Microwaves** and other man-made forms of electromagnetic fields (EMF) which are collectively called 'non-ionizing radiation' (a physics definition that is misleading in biology) have been rapidly increasing in human exposure due to increased electrification of our lives.

Just think of how many electronic gadgets and electrical appliances your house-hold used, say in the 1980s, if you are old enough to reflect on life at the time. Realisation about the toxicity of these common exposures made me extremely concerned and I couldn't help being worried – particularly for the children – humanity's biggest asset.

Dr. Milton Zaret MD, a military microwave research pioneer in the USA, was the first medical doctor to testify in the US Congress on the hazards of microwave radiation (9th March, 1973) and I share an excerpt from his testimony:

> "There is a clear, present and ever-increasing danger to the entire population of our country from exposure to the entire non-ionizing portion of the electromagnetic spectrum. The dangers cannot be overstated because most non-ionizing radiation injuries occur covertly, usually do not become

manifest until after latent periods of years, and when they do become manifest, the effects are seldom recognized."

I have been standing on the shoulders of giants in scientific/medical research who have completed meticulous investigations for many decades, and published to share that essential knowledge for health and regulatory agencies to use, for public health protection. I was baffled by regulatory failure in the West and a surprising, more protective approach by Russia and the former Soviet-bloc countries.

Scientific evidence indicating serious harm to mental and physical health from exposure to microwave radiation and other EMFs has been largely ignored by the Western and international health agencies, all the way to the World Health Organization (WHO) and Western regulatory bodies. Instead of following the much needed 'Precautionary Principle' and guiding the public to reduce exposure, government agencies and their advisory professional bodies; non-governmental organisation (NGOs), all with abbreviated big names that people call "alphabet agencies", such as the Australian Radiation Protection & Nuclear Safety Agency (ARPANSA) and the International Commission on Non-Ionization Radiation Protection (ICNIRP), have been parroting empty statements of safety. A common claim is *"There is no consistent scientific evidence of harm."* Yet, they continue to secure their funding declaring the importance of research and promising to expand research – forever keeping the unsuspecting public and the medical professionals misled. The intensifying microwave irradiation of even unborn babies in utero has been happening without the knowledge of the medical fraternity – guardians of health who are meant to protect public health.

**Ignorance about the harm caused by wireless radiation on the part of health professionals is shocking, and the alphabet agencies and their advisory NGOs should be held responsible for misleading them.**

As I write this Foreward, in December of 2024, after devoting the last 14 years to research in this field, and to educate medical professionals and the public (facing much resistance from the alphabet agencies and the industry), I would say "Unfathomable conflicts of interests of the military-industrial complex". Chery, in this book, talks about "Profits @ Any Cost" which is clearly a major driver, and I must emphasise the other P at any cost – Power! This "flying blind" exercise towards the ominous digital surveillance state through the Internet-of-Things (IoT) and the Internet-of-Living Things (IoLT) is evidently about control of the human population.

After serendipitously becoming educated about the health hazards of man-made EMR (in contrast, natural EMR from sunlight, is life giving) in early 2012, and unexpectedly curing my younger son from chronic multiple neuro-immune diseases, simply by eliminating toxic levels of RF-EMR at home (note; a baby monitor and a cordless phone by his bedside were the main culprits), I was like a magnet to the science on this topic. As a medical Mum, it was just awful to be medicating a child from infancy when you know there are always adverse effects of pharmaceutical products. So, it was truly exhilarating when my son's health problems resolved and we could stop long-term medications.

I was intensely studying research publications and communicating with experts who had conducted medical research. I clearly remember having an informative telephone conversation with Dr. Bruce Hocking, the former Chief Medical Officer of Telstra (from its Telecom Australia days). Hocking led research into investigating health impacts of wireless radiation in the early 1990s and found strong evidence of RF-EMR exposure associated with increased incidence of cancer. His findings and insistence on the precautionary approach didn't serve his career well. His position was made redundant. In private practice, he conducted tests on people who were claiming to develop neurological symptoms such as headaches upon use of mobile phones and published empirical evidence of bona *fide* physiological responses. He also supported community campaigns to keep mobile phone base stations (MPBS) or masts away from sensitive places like schools. By the time I talked to him, he had gone quiet on this topic in public, but he was pleased to hear about my interest in the science and shared very important scientific information with me – even asking me to keep him informed on my scientific findings. However, he said in a very disheartened tone *"You can't win with that industry"*. These words have echoed in me over the years. He was just one of the real medical experts (most people in powerful positions with regards to control of EMR are not proper health experts) who tried to establish evidence based public exposure regulation of wireless radiation, albeit unsuccessfully. I have listened to many experts expressing sheer frustration about the unethical manipulations, sabotage of the evidence of harm and the censorship of honest scientists.

**I urge you to check out the 'International EMF Scientist Appeal'.** [1] The International Scientist Appeal was sent to: **His Excellency Antonio Guterres, Secretary-General of the United Nations; Honorable Dr. Tedros Adhanom Ghebreyesus, Director-General of the World Health Organization; Honorable Inger Andersen, Executive Director of the U.N. Environment Programme; U.N. Member Nations**

"Between 1949 and 1962, everything we needed to know about microwaves was known and published. By 1962, all of the dangers, all of the hazards were known…the brain at that time had been studied for brain waves and microwaves could be used to penetrate the brain and cause behavioural changes…A statement was made in 1962 by the government that all birth defects, organs, whole organisms, all cells, brain function, all emotions, all moods could be altered, changed and destroyed … Microwaves then, as now, were used as stealth weapons before they became cell phones" (excerpts from a presentation by Barrie Trower, former UK Government microwave/electronic warfare expert of the Royal Navy, 3rd February, 2020).[2]

Similar to Chery's experience with politicians, I too found them to be mostly disingenuous and useless. A few that took some interest proved to be powerless to make a change – and they went quiet. Like Chery, I too thought that the Greens Party would take an interest in protecting life on earth from electromagnetic pollution, but I was mistaken. They and the associated environmental lobbies that are beating drums about the doubling of life-giving gas carbon dioxide ($CO_2$) in the atmosphere since 1950s, calling it "pollution", did not want to pay any attention to the increase by a quintillion times ($10^{18}$) of this entirely man-made toxic form of radiation, over the same period. I urge you to see details in my Lancet Planetary Health communication titled *Planetary electromagnetic pollution: it is time to assess its impact.* [3] This double-standard is due to a hidden destructive agenda in the background that has hijacked our system, along with the scientific institutions that were once credible. In order to find truths that pose existential threats, one has to do one's own research beyond the mainstream narratives. It takes moral courage to do so.

## A Sad Truth

I have seen many EMR canaries fade away from society and some have tragically passed away quite young. There is unfortunately a terrible stigma attached to this genuine environmental syndrome. People who are suffering from these modern toxic radiation exposures are ridiculed as "Tin Foil Hatters" – even by mainstream media. What a way to "**gaslight**" people (a new word I learned during the Covid-19 pandemic years; meaning a form of psychological manipulation, i.e., misleading someone into doubting reality) and suppress a health problem caused by the mighty military-industrial complex! Although the term "electromagnetic hypersensitivity" (EHS) is commonly used now, which tends to put the emphasis on the person for being too sensitive, we should continue the conventional term 'microwave sickness' which properly recognises the agent that causes the sickness. Carefully crafted words are used in this field to keep the public calm – for example, the traditional term 'electromagnetic radiation' is now largely replaced by 'electromagnetic energy'.

Not only is Chery an investigative canary; she is an intelligent and courageous woman with determination to overcome life's challenges. She has managed to recuperate from severe microwave sickness. Her 'Top Tips for being healthier and smarter than your smartphone' are absolutely essential if you are determined to protect your health in the 21st century.

I congratulate Chery on writing this informative book to wake up the sleeping masses from their trans-like state over their shiny digital screens. We can use efficient communications and use the internet safely via wired connections before the current mental health crisis escalates humanity into a zombie state.

Unless ordinary people share the knowledge and empower communities to take protective action without further delay, we're heading for a catastrophic situation due to blinding technocracy on steroids. When the human society is plagued by mental health problems at an unprecedented scale, our ability to think through the problems and take necessary action weakens. May sanity prevail! And you, the reader, realise that we must put a stop to this dangerous microwave irradiation we're subjected to, just like guineapigs in a lab experiment.

Be empowered with this essential knowledge to survive the digital age.

With my best wishes,

Dr. Priyanka (Pri) Bandara

Freelance medical researcher/educator, Sydney, Australia

(Links to Dr. Bandara's research can be found in the Endnotes and available on www.wellintent.net.)

# CHAPTER 1
# EXPOSING SYSTEMIC LIES, FRAUD AND PROFITS @ ANY COST

*"All truth passes through three stages. First, it is ridiculed. Second, it is violently opposed. Third, it is accepted as being self-evident."*

- Arthur Schopenhauer, Philosopher

## CANARIES EXPOSE THE TRUTH, THE WHOLE TRUTH AND NOTHING BUT THE TRUTH

What if most of what you've been led to believe is true, is actually a lie? Would you want to know the truth or at least seek a second opinion. If you or a loved one has been given a potential life-ending diagnosis, would you want to know about alternative actions you could take, to survive? What if there was a way to identify causes instead of cures. What if truth has been hidden from you, because telling the truth doesn't make money. It may seem incomprehensible that people would do that, but as you read the stories and follow the evidence in this book, you'll discover what I suggest is true. It's time to learn, from those that experience first-hand the effects and fallout, of the crimes committed by wealthy elites that control the world, for their benefit, not yours. Without this knowledge you are snookered by lack of seeing, mostly because you've been kept in the dark. With help from many canaries and truthers I'll help you gain an understanding of how crimes against humanity are carried out, why you need to be concerned and how to take appropriate action.

Canaries are the evidence of crimes being committed by those in power. Crimes you may not be aware of. Canaries harmed by invisible frequencies have been warning the world for a long time. Their voices have been smothered intentionally. Some canaries are fact-checkers, some are critical thinkers and some don't survive. Critical thinkers do their homework and attempt to tell the world what they find, which often comes at a great cost. I discovered scientists and organisations, funded by multinational companies I call Profits @ Any Cost, have no morals, ethics, heart or soul. Critical thinker Vandana Shiva, author of *Oneness vs the 1%* [4] exposed the billionaires who fund philanthropic capitalism using copious amounts of money, raked in by immoral means. Shiva identifies how the billionaires are connected and highlights their devious ways, never reported in the main stream media. Instead, they are painted as do-gooders like Bill Gates, and Mark Zuckerberg, and promoted as leaders to look up to. In reality, the money-making machine orchestrated by Profits @ Any Cost have put humanity on the precipice of destruction, resulting in a gigantic loss of human life and an even greater loss of human potential. Shiva's book is not the first book to expose the truth, but it is a good one. More will be revealed to understand how they've mastered the art of corruption and coverup, and why an alternative education can help save lives. Sadly, some people can't be saved because they don't want to be saved. Humans are creatures of habit and many don't believe they need to change anything, least of all their mind or their habits. I guess time will tell.

When I first ventured into the unknown world of alternative education, or what I call the secret sphere of influence, Eben Pagan, founder of Accelerate High Growth Business Training, told me to watch the Matrix movie. I didn't watch it, I read reviews and decided **science fiction was not my cup of tea. Here's an outline of the plot I found on IMDb, a website that reviews and rates movies:**

"Have you ever had a dream that you were so sure was real? What if you couldn't awaken? How would you know the difference between dream and reality? When a beautiful stranger (Carrie-Anne Moss) leads computer hacker Neo (Keanu Reeves) to a forbidding underworld, he discovers the shocking truth--the life he knows is the elaborate deception of an evil cyber-intelligence. Neo joins legendary and dangerous rebel warrior Morpheus (<u>Laurence Fishburne</u>) in the battle to destroy the illusion enslaving humanity." [5]

Instead of watching the Matrix movie I watched *The Real Matrix,* a documentary on the Iraq war, exposing lies and deceit of untold actions upon innocent people in Iraq. It showed how the USA government staged the war, and covered up what was really going on. What I didn't know at the time, about the Matrix movie, was an option to take the red pill or the blue pill. Taking the red pill would take you out of the matrix (mechanisms of control), and taking the blue pill would keep you firmly believing in a web of lies. A few years later I took the red pill.

You are about to get red pilled. That means you will become, if you read the whole book, an awakened individual who comprehends the truth. You'll understand how Profits @ Any Cost have brainwashed and manipulated our minds, our beliefs and influenced and infiltrated all the systems of the world, for their own benefit. You have to be willing to take the red pill; it can't be forced upon you. It's similar to the four stages of learning noted below. You choose to learn when it suits you. Every stage is a choice you make after stage 1.

**Stage 1.  Unconscious incompetence** – you are unaware you don't know.

**Stage 2.  Conscious incompetence** – you become aware but you need to learn how

**Stage 3.  Conscious competence** – you are aware and you practice to get better

**Stage 4.  Unconscious competence** – you automatically know and you automatically do everything without having to think about it.

Getting to stage 4 takes effort, consistency and practice, similar to learning to drive a vehicle.

**Stage 1.**  is when you're unaware you need to learn how to drive.

**Stage 2.**  happens when you're old enough, depending on your situation, and you realise learning to drive is necessary, if you want the freedom to go anywhere you please.

**Stage 3.**  happens when you start to drive on your own without supervision.

**Stage 4.**  happens after you've been driving for a few years and you do everything automatically, without thinking about it.

Creating a multi-million-dollar trucking business will take more skills, and greater will and determination, at stage 3. As will becoming an unconsciously competent smart user of technology. Developing skills to become a critical thinker are honed in the doing stage.

This book is an investigation to find the truth, hidden in plain sight, but invisible to an untrained mind. You will find gems of wisdom throughout the book, and I've already left some, so take notes, or use sticky notes. If you'd like to identify the critical thinking that's required to solve the manipulation mystery it will take time. With a bit of effort by the end of this book you will have conscious competence, sufficient enough to save your life, like I did. If you'd like to reach the unconscious competence level of learning, you'll need every ounce of curiosity you've got, and an open mind, which is the opposite of blinkered thinking. Commonsense is not that common, even though it can be developed over time. Instead of jumping to conclusions too early, stop and think things through using logical reasoning. Invest time in learning to listen with intent to learn more (from sources without a conflict of interest), rather than reacting to something you're unaware of. When at first something doesn't make sense, give it time, it may be because it's in conflict with a prearranged education system designed by Profits @ Any Cost. I've included some surprises. Well, they were surprises when I first heard about them, so I hope you enjoy learning to think differently, because the aim is, to win the game of life.

## It's a Mad MAD World

MAD stands for Mutual Assured Destruction, a term I learned from Alex Collier, illuminating how secret groups collaboratively control the systems of governance, to intentionally carry out dirty deeds on innocent men, women and children worldwide. Canaries expose one method of destruction and truthers, aware of corruption, shine light on masterful manipulations, previously unseen and unknown by the majority of the world's population.

More about secret groups later. First, I believe it's necessary to give Canaries a voice, because they need your help to enlighten more people, regarding the harm caused by man-made electromagnetic frequencies. They have first-hand experience dealing with the health effects, denial of justice and mis-treatment by those in power. Their stories never make the mainstream news, and you need to understand why. This is your first clue to finding the villains who have engineered the systems to manipulate and control the masses.

I uncover proof, identify the lying liars and shine a light on what most people can't see because it's undetectable, covered up by a plague of corruption. This is a guide, if you want one; to dodge an invasive enemy, normally invisible to a human mind, and unable to be detected by unsuspecting people, without help from an expert investigator.

You will learn how mind control works and discover how they manipulate the science, the medical system, education system, legal system, political system, control our beliefs via education and the media. Are the villains connected? Absolutely. You'll see for yourself, if you're willing to let go of what you believe to be true. What I didn't know before, but I'm aware of now, is how the systems of power are designed to ensure you follow a false narrative, to boost Profits @ Any Cost multi-national businesses that benefit from technology and the harm it causes. Concealing the truth ensures they maintain control. Revealing the truth decreases their control. By the end of this book, you'll see the bleedingly obvious truth; how they've pulled it off, and you'll gain skills to protect yourself.

Those in charge use paid propaganda in the mainstream media (TV, news programs, radio and newspapers). They manipulate information to keep you trapped in a web of deceit and misinformation. Make room in your mind for an alternative education. It's the only way to wise-up to the network of schemes holding everyone's attention and perception. This is the Matrix I mentioned earlier.

George, who you'll meet shortly, is a like-minded canary I connected with through a social media EHS support group he manages. We discussed the lack of understanding and complexities of EMF exposure, and I asked him if I could tell his story to help expose the truth, and why it must be told to help others that may be suffering but have no idea why. Hold on to your hat, it's going to be a roller coaster of emotions, especially if you have no idea you've been lied to. This is a detective story of enormous proportions, not science fiction, not fake news and definitely not a conspiracy theory; it's a real investigation into crimes against humanity. A conspiracy is not a theory if it's proved to be true. According to Zero Hedge, the term Conspiracy Theory was created by the CIA in 1967 as a way to discredit anyone who dared to challenge their official version of the truth. [6] Patricia Burke posted a very interesting blog on Natural Blaze covering this topic.[7] Stick around you'll learn a thing or two, or three, or more. Your mind will expand and I guarantee, it never goes back to its original size.

Prior to studying Building Biology, I had no idea EHS, or canaries existed, or that mam-made frequencies affect every system in your body, and every body. Only when a canary tells their story do you realise the systems need to change, not from the top down but from the bottom up. We, the people, are the solution only most people don't know it.

## George is a canary of long standing

When George told me his history, of the lack of support from the medical system and his attempts to expose the truth, I realised it showcased how people in the health system have no idea microwave frequencies used in new technology are dangerous. George's story also proves the harm caused by RFR exposure is not a new phenomenon of the 21st century.

George served in the Australian army from 1959-1980, and was in charge of a Signals Communications Troop from 1968-1969 in Vietnam. Prior to this one year in Vietnam, George was healthy and physically fit, with not a worry in the world.

While in Vietnam George used a powerful 1,000-watt E513 radio, inside a communications tent. When he began to feel ill, he called it his "silent illness" because no health professional could identify what it was.

*Above: George in front of the radio tower, used to transmit signals back to Australia from Vietnam in 1968-1969.*

George said *"I felt like I had ants crawling all over me."*

George's health effects increased when he returned to Australia. He suffered continual flu-like illness, painful glands, cold sweats, fatigue, difficulty with memory and concentration and aches and pains in joints and muscles. Doctors prescribed antibiotics, anti-depressants and other medications but nothing worked. They had no idea what he was suffering from.

Chemicals and insecticides sprayed in Vietnam may have contributed to his health effects but they didn't explain his persistent lack of concentration, memory loss, severe headaches, migraines, numbness and tingling or dizziness to the point of fainting. From 1984 – 1997 George had no inkling of the primary cause of his ill health.

An amazing thing happened in 1997. George and his wife Joan moved to Tasmania, an island state, south of the Australian mainland, where his health improved. The location away from mobile phone coverage and electrical transmission lines allowed his body to recover. At that time, George was unaware of the reasons for the improvement. George's symptoms disappeared, and he began experiencing good health for the first time since 1969.

George and Joan, returned to mainland Australia in 2000, with a plan to explore the island continent but unfortunately his symptoms returned almost instantly. It wasn't until they were touring in a caravan that the cause became obvious. George was ok when they were travelling until Joan used her mobile phone, which triggered the tingling and burning sensations again. When they camped in powered caravan sites, George's symptoms escalated.

Within twelve months all the health effects returned, the same as he'd experienced in Vietnam. In 2004 George uncovered the culprit. He read an article on microwave illness confirming exposure to microwave wireless technology caused multiple health effects, and was known to cause harm as far back as 1950.

Microwave radio frequencies are a band of frequencies on the radio frequency spectrum used for communications. The powers-that-be have known about the health effects for a long time and governments have allowed the roll out, and profiteering, of more and more radiofrequencies in the form of 3G, 4G and 5G over the last thirty years. This means they have intentionally rolled out third, fourth and fifth generation technology, knowing the harm it causes. This is where we go down the rabbit hole of lack of truth connected to lack of integrity, morals, and ethics. It's a big rabbit hole.

High exposure and longevity of exposure to radio frequency radiation caused George's health effects, labelled as electrical hypersensitivity (EHS) in the scientific literature. EHS happens because of bio-accumulation, which is a build-up of unnatural man-made frequencies in the body causing multiple health effects.

George and I discussed many of the issues exposed in this book and we've both alerted the authorities, to no avail, which you'll hear about shortly. In addition, you'll learn how we fight the somewhat silent fight. First, I'll share some studies that have conveniently been ignored, which is the first indication that coverups happen at the highest level.

## EVENTS THAT SHOULD HAVE RUNG ALARM BELLS 80 YEARS AGO

It would be natural to think EHS or microwave frequency poisoning (real term) is a new phenomenon, but it is not. I came across articles that expose how man-made electromagnetic fields and frequencies have been identified as harmful to humans for over 100 years.

A Royal Commission Report [8] dated 1907 was produced after Toronto switchboard workers went on strike due to injuries received from working conditions and pressure to work long hours. Multiple health effects identified in the report, often left women unable to work. At that time, the biological effects were called Neurasthenia, a name coined by American George Beard in 1868, a physician that described an illness often affecting telegraph line workers and later affecting telephone switchboard operators, exposed to electromagnetic frequencies (EMF) from the equipment they were using.

Harold J. Cook, et al. from the University of Michigan, produced a report in 1979; **Early Research on the Biological Effects of Microwave Radiation: 1940-1960** [9] stating that radar development began early in World War II, and concerns arose that this new energy classified as microwave radiation, could potentially have detrimental effects on personnel. In the past, experts suggested the energy levels of microwaves produced at that time, were not sufficient to cause harmful effects, even though the health effects of radiation were known as far back as 1906. This means they knew in 1979 of the earlier reported effects and of the detrimental effects on military personnel in 1960.

## Health implications of long-term exposure to electrosmog

You may think the reports above are isolated cases, however research in Russia proved the harm from new technology was not isolated to Canada or USA. German Professor Karl Hecht formulated a Brochure Series of the Competence Initiative for the Protection of Humanity, the Environment and Democracy; produced in collaboration with multiple medical associates and expert advisory board members, which highlighted the health effects of wireless communication technologies. An English edition of this German paper was not produced until 2012. The title image for this document depicts radar victims and widows of deceased radar victims, demonstrating for their rights, and against the violation of their human dignity in a state of law (Hect Archives). [10.]

Hecht Series, Brochure 6 covers the common misconceptions about the effects of electromagnetic fields and the long-term exposure effects of radio-frequency and microwave radiation in humans between 1960 and 1996.

**Hecht outlines the ignorance and inhumane treatment of persons with electromagnetic hypersensitivity and disabilities caused by exposure to radio frequency radiation (RFR).**

Hecht discusses comprehensive assessments of 878 Russian studies between 1960 and 1997. A long list of experts suggests *"to ignore the connection between microwave technologies from the past and present and that they are not connected to health effects today, is like burying your head in the*

*sand."* **Tactics by political officialdom are crimes against humanity.**
Hecht states *"Health is a Basic Human Right."* He also stated that *"restricting truth was part of a totalitarian atrocity committed by dictators not that long ago."*

> Hecht quote: 'New diseases are emerging. The incidence of known diseases keeps increasing, sometimes dramatically so; electromagnetic hypersensitivity, multiple chemical sensitivity, noise sensitivity, tinnitus, and auditory processing disorders, depression, sleeplessness, helplessness syndrome and serious consequences of distress on many others."

Law makers, around the world including Australia, Canada, UK, Europe and North America, fail to help those affected. Governments and heads of the medical establishment hide the truth. Medical education is lacking with doctors' mis-diagnosing and mis-treating those affected. Often, offering medications that do nothing more than mask symptoms or make them worse.

Great harm is done by failing to recognise the biological effects and even more harm when the people affected are shunned by family, co-workers, doctors, media and the telecom industry; denied claims by insurance companies and the legal system for compensation; and being told their symptoms are imagined and they should see a psychiatrist.

EMF Wise, a website dedicated to safe EMF, [11] produced a worldwide awareness timeline from 2000-2012 including: USA, Austria, Italy, Canada, India, Israel, Europe, Sweden, Russia, Spain, Belgium, Liechtenstein, and France. Taiwan noted concerns and took some action: USA and Australia's policy makers and industry experts have done nothing. Quite the opposite in fact. Professor Rodney Croft, head of the Australian Radiation Protection and Nuclear Safety Agency (ARPANSA - the agency responsible for RFR safety) and member of the International Commission on Non-Ionizing Radiation Protection (ICNIRP) - who has a PhD in psychology, not medicine or biology - stated *"there is no established, consistent evidence of harm."* ICNIRP is responsible for setting safety guidelines for all RFR levels worldwide.

ARPANSA is funded by the Australian Government to ensure Australian's have safe levels of exposure from all forms of radiation. This statement on the ARPANSA website indicates they have no concerns about RFR transmissions: "Conclusion; There is no established scientific evidence that the use of mobile phones causes any health effects…ARPANSA will continue to review the research into potential health effects of RF EME emissions from mobile phones and other devices in order to provide accurate and up-to-date advice." [12] [13] According to ARPANSA who follow ICNIRP guidelines, everyone is safe. Others have proved that is not the case.

## Things that make you go hmmm!

The Environmental Health Trust (EHT), an organisation, founded by Dr Devra Davis, an epidemiologist, toxicologist, safe EMF advocate and author of several books on environmental hazards, has been raising awareness about the impacts of cell phone radiation and other wireless technologies since 2007. [14] EHT wrote a letter to President Biden, in 2021 expressing the urgent need to evaluate the human health and environmental impact of 5G and the proliferation of wireless networks. Previously, in 2019, US medical professionals sent a letter to President Trump calling for urgent action on 5G and wireless networks. [15]

In 2019 EHT took legal action against the U.S. federal government for failing to properly review its laws on wireless radiation exposure. EHT won the case. From the EH Trust website: "United States Court of Appeals for the District of Columbia Circuit judges in favor of environmental health groups and petitioners; finds FCC violated the Administrative Procedure Act and failed to respond to comments on environmental harm." [16] An EHT presentation on YouTube by Devra Davis, presents history of cell phones and the reasons FCC standards are no longer relevant. [17]

You would think a win in court would change things, sadly not. Even though the EH Trust successfully identified the FCC regulatory standards did not protect people from harmful radiofrequency radiation, they have not changed their stance or standards.

## From the EHTrust.org website 2021: Facts

The court found the FCC ignored numerous organizations, scientists and medical doctors who called on them to update limits and the court found the FCC failed to address these issues:[18]

- impacts of long-term wireless exposure
- impacts to children,
- the testimony of people injured by wireless radiation,
- impacts to wildlife and the environment
- impacts to the developing brain and reproduction.

## FCC website 2024 - Blatant lies in plain sight:

What you will find, is a total disrespect of the rights of the people to a safe environment. I found this statement on the FCC website in 2024:

> While the FCC has continuously monitored research and conferred with experts in this field, and is confident in its RF exposure guidelines and the soundness of the basis for its rules, it is a matter of good government to periodically reexamine regulations and their implementation.

EH Trust won the case in 2019 but in 2025 FCC still denies the truth. Nothing has changed. There is no justice to be found in the legal system. [19]

Sadly, the Australia government and telecommunication industry follow the same song sheet as the USA, supporting denial of truth and denial of justice. Instead, the government supports the telecommunications industry in the rollout of 5G across Australia against people's wishes. This is not democracy; this is protection of Profits @ Any Costs, bordering on insanity. Here's why.

**A Parliamentary Inquiry into 5G in Australia** identifies brilliantly, the total denial of evidence of harm and the totalitarian dictatorship of government against the people of Australia. [20] The 2019 parliamentary inquiry received 538 submissions, with many people calling on a suspension of 5G technology until sufficient testing for safety was completed. The submissions are still available online. You may think this is not many submissions, but how many people in Australia knew the inquiry was taking place? I imagine - only those that had been advised and had a vested interest. I knew because the Building Biology community and the College of Environmental Studies advised me to take a look. Many experts and people affected by electromagnetic radiation stated their case by posting submissions. Does the government care about the people - I think not. A pattern is emerging where the wishes and needs of the people are being wilfully ignored. Further on you may begin to understand why, but first let's look at the governing bodies and the amalgamation of lies and misrepresentation of facts. In Chapter 2, we'll look at the health effects, under Evidence of Harm, to gauge whether you need to be concerned enough to act.

## ESSENTIAL READING: ORGANIZATIONS UNDER THE SPOT LIGHT

Governing bodies and controlling organisations are in bed together. They scratch each other's back and spin the same lies. Humanity is kept in the dark, to ensure control of the masses. I stand with the true independent scientific researchers, attempting to right this enormous injustice, by shining light on the truth.

Let's start with who provides the scientific advice to world governments to protect the people from radiation. That would be ICNIRP, [21] the International Commission on Non-Ionizing Radiation Protection. They declare they are an independent non-profit organisation providing scientific advice and guidance on the health and environmental effects of non-ionising radiation (NIR) to protect people and the environment from detrimental NIR exposure. They are funded by governments, and likely the telecommunication industry they support. ICNIRP doesn't protect the people or the environment, they protect Profits @ Any Cost, the telecommunications industry and governments worldwide that choose to hijack the truth. The FCC in the USA and ARPANSA use ICNIRP guidelines to set safety standards that suit industry. They do not support your state of health.

Who supports who? The World Health Organization (WHO), part of the United Nations, declare they work to promote health and keep the world safe from harm. Even Wikipedia supports the WHO, stating it is a specialised agency of the United Nations, responsible for international public health.

You may think these organisations have not received the memo that people are being harmed by EMF exposures but you would be wrong to think that. The Hecht Brochure, and the International Scientist Appeal: A statement by Scientists (worldwide) calling for Protection from Non-ionizing Electromagnetic Field Exposure – were both issued to:

**His Excellency Antonio Guterres, Secretary-General of the United Nations; Honorable Dr. Tedros Adhanom Ghebreyesus, Director-General of the World Health Organization; Honorable Inger Andersen, Executive Director of the U.N. Environment Programme; U.N. Member Nations**

Now we are starting to see how they control the masses. United Nations, ICNIRP, WHO, Wikipedia, FCC, ARPANSA and world governments dictate what the Profits @ Any Cost want you to hear, not what you need to know. They follow the same game plan, pervert the truth and support industry to ensure the truth is never divulged. The general public have no idea they can't be trusted.

## Who can you trust?

First, we have to trust canaries because human experience is the greatest scientific test ever invented. We are intelligent, supernatural beings with the most advanced biological system that doctors cannot equal. Example: when you break a bone, say it's your leg, you go to hospital, your leg is put in a cast and you're sent home. Within six weeks you go back to have the cast removed and your leg has mended. The doctors, unless you need surgery and plates and screws to secure the bones together, plays no part in the process of repair. Your body knows what to do.

YES, we've just found the expert you need to rely on and it's inside of you! Natural intelligence is without any doubt the most amazing thing. Without people realising it, the power-hungry elites through the indoctrination of the systems, including the medical establishment have dumbed down the population so much so that people rarely question their own biological authority.

We need to unravel the concocted multi-billion-dollar propaganda-for-hire public relations (PR) industry to reveal the truth and identify who the true heroes of our time are. I hope you're ready for exposure to the dogma of accepted beliefs and indoctrination by a group of self-appointed authoritarians. You are about to learn what they have been serving up to us from day one. Prepare to take another red pill.

## Microwave Warfare

Barrie Trower, a long-term activist, trained at the UK government's microwave warfare establishment for the Royal Navy, has been sharing his knowledge and warning people for a long time. [22] In an article Barrie prepared for the King of Botswana, in April 2010, he describes the outcomes of microwave warfare. [23]

This is an extract from Barrie's article:

> Debriefing spies during The Cold War extended my military education into the full diversity of stealth microwave warfare and communication systems. I was previously aware of reports concerning dead birds in and around communication

bases. On examination these birds were found to be cooked. Microwaves are the preferred medium for communication, over radiowaves, due to their superior penetrative properties and ability to carry more information.

Our Government and the International Commission for Non-Ionizing Radiation (ICNIRP) classify microwaves as electromagnetic waves from 300 M Hz to 300 G Hz. (NRPB 2004). To my knowledge, 'microwave or radiowave sickness' was first reported in August 1932 with the symptoms of: severe tiredness, fatigue, fitful sleep, headaches, intolerability and high susceptibility to infection (Hecht, 2007).

Barrie has attended many UK and international meetings, conferences and advised some Parliamentary committees and decision-making bodies that often refer to the WHO and ICNIRP as to the concern of microwave irradiation. If decision making bodies refer to WHO and ICNIRP, why isn't the message getting through. This is starting to look like a plot to inflict enormous harm on humanity, but surely normal people in charge of policy would not let this happen? Hmmm. Let's find out.

## Political Deep Fake Democracy

In February 2020 I wrote a letter and presented it in person, with evidence to an Australian Politician, a member of the Greens Political Party in the Victorian Legislative Assembly. The MP is a former general practitioner, and medical researcher with a PhD on the epidemiology of sexually transmitted infections. He is the Greens spokesperson for Health, Justice, Integrity and Science. During the meeting I presented scientific research on two subjects of inquiry and explained my professional opinion based on lived experience.

1.  Parliamentary Inquiry into Biotoxin-Related Illness, [24] and

2.  Rollout of 5G in Australia.[25]

My first concern related to the instance of mould in water-damaged homes that is not being address appropriately at government level. Many people are mis-diagnosed with chronic fatigue syndrome, autoimmune disorders or multiple system dysfunction. Most doctors are not trained in environmental exposures and never ask their patients about their environment or what they have been exposed to. My own experience proves this point, and I'll tell you about it later. In my letter I provided the following information.

Dr. Richie Shoemaker, a mould specialist in the USA, classified CIRS (chronic inflammatory response syndrome) or WDB (water damaged building) illness as biotoxin illness that severely affects 24% of the population. Genetically susceptible people do not make antibodies to deal with the biotoxins. This means the biotoxins cause continuing unregulated production of cytokines (immune system signalling molecules) causing high levels of inflammation which leads to damage of multiple systems in the body, including the gastrointestinal system, the central nervous system and cross the blood brain barrier causing neurological damage.

**Mould spores in the air, are breathed in, causing an autonomic nervous system response. Unrelenting cold and flu symptoms are an attempt by your immune system to remove the mould spores (biological-toxins) from the body.**

Biotoxins are not one particular toxin but a combination of endotoxins entering the body via inhalation, food, water or tick/bug bite. Shoemaker and Maizel (2009) [26] indicate over 90% of patients present with fatigue and multi-system and multi-symptom illness. According to Dr Shoemaker (2010) [27] the adverse health effects caused by these biotoxins include impaired nerve cell function, chronic pain, sleep disturbance, gastrointestinal problems, flu-like symptoms; muscle aches, unstable temperature, difficulty concentrating and patients have difficulty recovering from illness.

The second parliamentary inquiry of concern involves the rollout of 5G in Australia. In my letter to the Greens MP, I address the issues of 5G, and the increase of frequencies on the radiofrequency spectrum. I explained my position and professional experience in my letter. Here's an extract:

> As a building biologist I am called to conduct audits or assessments on homes where people, often children, are extremely sick and fail to get better. People today are exposed to environmental toxins that the medical profession are not addressing, possibly because they are unaware of the health effects or lack the time to devote to education on biological effects of man-made electrical pollution.
>
> Exposure to more and more electromagnetic radiation (EMR) from wireless communications...in the built environment is having devastating consequences on our population and on me.
>
> I have become extremely electrically sensitive since moving to Melbourne and can now relate to the health effects experienced by my clients.
>
> The best way to explain the seriousness of this condition is to say that my body is aging at a rate of knots that is scaring me. Sufficiently so that we have moved a number of times to reduce exposure to wireless transmissions and tried various ways to shield myself from EMR and reduce EMF in my home.
>
> Of great concern is the rollout of more EMR in the form of 5G which is the 5th Generation protocol for wireless communications. This will have devastating effects on the people of Australia.
>
> For your information I provide herewith, independent research on the health effects of EMF/EMR and a list of organisations worldwide opposed to the increase of satellites and expansion of 5G technology on an already overloaded radio frequency spectrum, specifically for, in my professional opinion, the control of people through technology and the focus on money and profits from selling more products and services.

> If the issue of health effects is not dealt with in an open and honest way the long-term health of our people is in jeopardy. And long-term could mean less than 10 years according to experts worldwide.
>
> Independent research has been carried out around the world and some countries have taken notice and reduced their exposure limits.

Included with my letter to the Greens MP, were two substantial documents containing significant independent research to support my case for a reduction in RF transmission starting immediately, and an awareness of the health effects caused by wireless technology.

One very significant document identified the danger to human health, titled the **Seletun Scientific Statement**, [28] produced by scientists led by Olle Johansson PhD., from Sweden's Karolinska Institute. Johansson recommended global governments adopt safe exposure standards and guidelines to reduce harmful levels of electromagnetic radiation. Johansson emphatically stated there is great risk to life due to the unchecked proliferation of wireless technology.

Additionally, the **BioInitiative Report 2012** produced by 29 authors from ten countries, ten holding medical degrees (MDs), 21 PhDs, and three MsC, MA or MPHs provides overwhelming evidence of harm. [29]

> The BioInitiative Report Preface states; The great strength of the BioInitiative Report is that it has been done independent of governments, existing bodies and industry professional societies that have clung to old standards. Precisely because of this, the BioInitiative Report presents a solid scientific and public health policy assessment that is evidence-based.

The BioInitiative Report 2012 containing around 1800 new studies on the bio-effects of electromagnetic fields and radiofrequency radiation clearly identifies adverse health effects from mobile phone masts (cell towers),

Wi-Fi, wireless utility 'smart' meters, and that regular mobile phone use can result in illness. Prolonged exposure disrupts homeostasis, which is the self-regulating process by which biological systems maintain stability, causing unstable biological conditions. Disruptions to homeostasis can lead to disease and death.

My letter to a Greens MP continued...

> Last year (2018) I joined The Greens because I believe the party holds similar values to myself and if we are to make Australia a better, smarter place to live we must be prepared to deal with these issues. I hope to be more involved in policy making that will initiate conversations among members to address these two difficult subjects with a goal of devising solutions to ensure our future is safe and we as a nation lead the way in sustainable development with a focus on life-long health and well-being. Yours faithfully.

## Lesson learned; don't trust Governments or politicians

How naïve was I. I thought if I joined the Greens Policy Conveners Committee and attended workshops on policy, which were think-tank sessions made up of, what seemed like, honest conscientious people wanting to make a difference, I'd be in the right place to initiate change. At the very next meeting I attended, along with the MP as co-ordinator, I brought up the subject of 5G, because we were talking about nuclear and radiation safety. The exact same government agency ARPANSA, that is the governing body responsible for radiation safety. When I mentioned 5G the MP immediately stopped any discussion on the matter saying it wasn't relevant at this time and continued with the meeting without letting me explain further. Wow, I was blown away by his disregard of the evidence and that he literally ignored all the scientific research I presented. I wasn't prepared for his negative response or his manipulation of conversation, because he'd seemed genuinely concerned during our meeting.

That was my big wake up to the fact politicians are complicit in crimes against humanity and we as normal folk, are literally stopped from telling the truth or having a say. Here is a well-educated politician, with a medical degree, that I thought would understand the science and immediately take action. Deceit is not limited to politicians.

My search to identify "how do I attack this problem" didn't stop there. I looked into the medical profession professional code of conduct, thinking maybe it's flawed. What I found was rather surprising and at one stage I believed the oath they take would hold power.

**The Australian Medical Association (AMA)** has adopted the World Medical Association's (WMA) Declaration of Geneva, the 2,500-year-old Hippocratic Oath for doctors to declare their commitment to their profession, their patients, and humanity. [30]

> **Declaration of Geneva (WMA, 2006)**
>
> At the time of being admitted as a member of the medical profession:
>
> I solemnly pledge to consecrate my life to the service of humanity;
>
> I will give to my teachers the respect and gratitude that is their due;
>
> I will practise my profession with conscience and dignity;
>
> The health of my patient will be my first consideration;
>
> I will respect the secrets that are confided in me, even after the patient has died;
>
> I will maintain, by all the means in my power, the honour and the noble traditions of the medical profession;
>
> My colleagues will be my sisters and brothers;
>
> I will not permit considerations of age, disease or disability, creed, ethnic origin, gender, nationality, political affiliation,

race, sexual orientation, social standing or any other factor to intervene between my duty and my patient;

I will maintain the utmost respect for human life;

I will not use my medical knowledge to violate human rights and civil liberties, even under threat;

I make these promises solemnly, freely and upon my honour.

An oath is normally a promise, a solemn declaration to fulfill a pledge. In all honesty, if the oath was in force, and acted upon we wouldn't have a problem. Obviously, many doctors (as you will learn shortly) don't practice what the AMA preaches.

I'm going to make an assumption here. Most doctors believe they are helping people get better. Some change their focus when they realise drugs don't work, or some realise exposing the truth gets them kicked off the medical register. One such doctor is Dr Charlie Teo, who spoke up about mobile phones causing brain tumours. Dr. Teo appeared on a 60 Minutes Report revealing the rise in brain tumours. [31] After that interview Dr. Teo was found guilty of unsatisfactory misconduct and banned from practicing in Australia. I listened to Dr. Teo on an EMF Summit justifiably expressing his concerns. The medical mafia do not want people knowing the truth, which means they will do anything to hide the truth. My understanding, after years of research, indicates it's the hierarchy of control, within the medical system that needs fixing. Dr. Teo is not the only one cast out of the system. More on that later. A very good example of how the system controls the narrative, is a statement by the (2020) Governments Chief Health Officer, Dr. Brendan Murphy, in a press release dated January 2020, to all Australians:

Title: Safety of 5G Technology

1. I'd like to reassure the community that 5G technology is safe.

2. The radio waves to which the general public is exposed from telecommunications are not hazardous to health.

3. There is no evidence telecommunications technologies, such as 5G, cause adverse health effects.

Chief Medical Officer, Dr Brendan Murphy, was the spokesperson in charge in Australia, when they rolled out Covid-19 restrictions and mandates, in the name of biosecurity, health and safety. I hope you are joining the dots, like I did. You can read a letter sent to Dr. Brendan Murphy by Environment & Communities Safe from Radiation Inc., on April 15, 2020, calling on the government to Cease and Desist, which was available on their website. The website doesn't seem to exist anymore. Luckily, I saved a copy and it is available on **www.wellintent.net/essential-reading**, [32] highlighting evidence provided to the Chief Health Officer and many other members of government and health officials. Basically, they can't say they don't know of the harm caused by EMF and radiofrequency radiation.

Good people all over the world are voicing their objections to exposure from harmful RF microwave radiation. Stop 5G groups, including the ones George and I are connected to, are not the only ones exposing the truth to people responsible for public safety. It seems we can't trust politicians, governments and Chief Medical Doctors, who appear to be psychopaths, (a normal person of good intent would not ignore the science). Who can we trust? You will find out, and it's better than you could ever imagine.

## THE MEDICAL SYSTEM IS A HARD NUT TO CRACK WITHOUT A SLEDGE HAMMER

Once upon a time, a long time ago I believed my GP (general practitioner) had the answers to health problems, only to find out I was wrong. GPs are not experts. It took me years to wake up to the fact that they fail to solve health issues, and instead, often create them. My personal experiences taught me many things my doctor didn't acknowledge. Your body knows there is something wrong, and it's telling you all the time by producing a sign that something is making you sick (a symptom). Many people and doctors, fail to understand the symptom is not the problem, and what you (and the doctor) need to find is the cause. A symptom is the way your body warns you something is making you sick. Symptoms get treated, causes do not, and it's looking like causes get covered up because treating symptoms makes more money.

I can't remember the year but it was around 2008 when I sought help from my doctor for a persistent cough that wouldn't go away. The feeling I had was a continual build-up of phlegm that trickled down my throat causing me to cough. My doctor prescribed an asthma medication through an inhaler. When I tried it, it nearly killed me. I had a reaction ten times worse than the cough. When I returned to the doctor, I told her I couldn't use the medication, because it produced a worse reaction than the cough, and her reply was *"sometimes you have to suffer the side effects or suffer the symptoms."* A lightbulb moment.

Not long after, when searching for some supplements to boost my immune system, I was approached by a lady herbalist. She asked me if she could help, and of course I said yes. She told me she had been a pharmacist before venturing into herbal medicine because of the benefits, and lack of side effects. We had a short conversation and she looked at my throat, my eyes, my hands and nails and suggested some tonics and some herbal remedies to try. Within two weeks my cough was gone and I was well again.

When I told my doctor I'd fixed the cough using herbal remedies, she did not want to know. What I didn't know at the time, but discovered during mould training at ACES was, I'd been exposed to mould working in a water-damaged building, and mould spores I'd been breathing in were the cause of the cough and respiratory problem. My immune system was working to eliminate the spores (biological toxins), unbeknown to me, and all it needed was a helping hand from nature.

### Symptoms are warning signs your body's natural intelligence is fighting for your life.

Another time in Port Melbourne, when I sought a solution for an infected toe. I asked a doctor if he knew anything about electrical hypersensitivity and he'd never heard of it, and didn't seem very interested in my profession.

He prescribed a topical antibiotic for my toe and I left him a paper on the effects of EMF and RF radiation. When I applied the topical antibiotic, I immediately felt nauseous so I stopped using it. I solved the skin infection by applying tea tree essential oil. GPs are trained by the medical system and many are unaware of the link between wireless radiation and environmental toxins causing illness and disease. Sadly, they are like macadamia nuts; they have a near impenetrable skull, due to programming. They are a hard nut to crack, and are often part of the problem, which I expose next.

## Social Exclusion due to Electrical Hypersensitivity

I believe one of the most comprehensive documents I've read in relation to the treatment, or mistreatment, of people with EHS, is a booklet about Social Exclusion due to Electromagnetic Pollution: A Belgian Perspective.

You will find an up-to-date account by Gérald Hanotiaux, of investigations commenced in June 2020, [33] of the effects of wireless radiation on electrically sensitive people; available on the Electrical Sensitivity UK website. People with EHS have to endure total exclusion from workplaces and society, and dealing with the effects is not simply a small inconvenience - the impact can be truly catastrophic. It is virtually impossible for people to find safe accommodation; therefore, many relocate to areas that have no internet or live in cars or caravans away from the maddening crowds. It is estimated 3.3 million people in France are affected and 573,000 in Belgium. This is not an insignificant portion of the population. This is similar to numbers in Canada, USA, UK and Australia, where between 5-10% of the population are significantly affected, and 30% are moderately affected.

In the section, *Encounters with the medical profession,* it appears some GPs are aware of EHS, and provide a medical certificate that is often the only support they get. A second group of doctors, say they know a little about the issues but there's not much they can do, sadly the third category react negatively...quite scandalously actually. Electrosensitive people have to conduct their own research ending in some people deciding not to talk to doctors, and in one testimony, the doctor thought it was a laughing matter. Lack of support from medical professionals can have dramatic consequences.

### *"Denial on the part of health professionals is itself a serious public health problem."*

Doctors are not the only problem; EHS people spoke of friends progressively distancing themselves from their electrosensitive friend. Some EHS people moved countless times to find a safe place to live, using up all their funds, and ending up homeless with nowhere to go. Some create their own bunker by painting the walls with shielding paint, only to find they cannot leave their bunker. One lady wanted to share her story to relay how complexly anti-constitutional it is that there is nowhere for people with EHS to live. She ended up in a camper van on a property in the middle of nowhere, because life in a city meant living with tachycardia, restlessness, chronic fatigue, and unbearable headaches.

### Covering as much of the country as they can with 5G, seems ludicrous.

**You may think not many people know about EHS, but that's not true.** ES-UK.info [34] is a website in the United Kingdom that addresses all issues related to electrical sensitivity and electrical hypersensitivity. Electrical Sensitivity UK, is a charity founded in 2003 supporting electro-sensitive people. Medical Advisors, Dr Erica Mallery-Blythe founder of PHIRE (Physicians' Health Initiative for Radiation and Environment), and Dr Dietrick Klinghardt, from the Klinghardt Institute, recognised internationally for special interests in chronic toxicity, (specifically lead, mercury, environmental pollutants and electromagnetic fields), along with Scientific Advisors; Dr Andrew Goldsworthy, Dr Magna Havas, Professor Olle Johansson, and Professor Denis Henshaw, provide much needed information and advice to address the ever-growing number of individuals affected by EMF/EMR.

## Multiple chemical sensitivity can be a precursor to electrical hypersensitivity

From an evaluation of 2018 cases of EHS, available from the European Clinical Trial Database, [35] Dominique Belpomme and Philippe Irigaray identified 25% of EHS cases were associated with multiple chemical sensitivity (MCS), of which 80.4% were female. It appears women are much more susceptible to EHS and/or MCS.

MCS link to EHS made complete sense to me. While I have never been diagnosed by a doctor as chemically sensitive, I've been sensitive to many things most of my life. It started with face cream I purchased in 1974. When my face turned bright red, I was told I was sensitive and had to use products labelled, 'for sensitive people'. I've reacted badly to medications, cleaning products and foods with additives like MSG for most of my life. I had a severe reaction to the contraceptive pill, which caused emotional imbalances and feelings of suicide, just before I was about to get married, which was a strange time to feel that life was not worth living. My doctor at the time told me to stop taking it and prescribed a mini pill that was less potent but it had to be taken at the same time every day, and was not to be missed. In my mid-thirties, after I had our fourth child, I had my tubes clamped and stopped taking the pill. I felt as if a weight had been lifted off me and I got my zest for life back; I was blissfully happy once more. Another lightbulb moment. The body knows medications are toxic.

EHS escalated my MCS, so much so I only need a whiff of a chemical and I start coughing, or get a headache or my stomach hurts. If I consume chemically loaded food, including wheat products containing Roundup Ready Wheat, a genetically modified organism (GMO), designed to be resistant to the herbicide Roundup, I am alerted immediately by gut pain. Glyphosate is the main ingredient in Roundup, originally produced by Monsanto. The additive 621 monosodium glutamate (MSG) flavour enhancer, added to sauces or take-away foods, causes diabolical gut pain and sometimes irritation in my mouth. My body will react immediately, with indigestion followed by back pain and muscle inflammation the following day. Removing contaminated manufactured foods from my diet and only using organic cleaning and personal care products has pretty much reduced my reaction to chemicals.

If doctors don't know about MCS and EHS or microwave radiation illness and chronic inflammatory response syndrome (CIRS) caused by mould growing in water-damaged buildings, how many other illnesses caused by environmental exposures are they mis-diagnosing. When they are treating the symptom and not the cause, they are totally ineffective at helping patients get better.

I must be clear; not all doctors fall under the category of big pharma-controlled GPs. Many doctors I have studied with are experts in their field and emergency medicine is necessary to save lives. If you were involved in a car accident, received burns or fell from a great height, you need emergency medical care to save your life. What I'm alluding to is the lack of education and lack of concern when doctors' patients don't get better, or they are on medication all their life but continue to suffer with poor health.

Big pharmaceutical companies make money when you're sick; not when you're well. The Rockefeller and Carnegie Foundations funded and controlled the modern medical system from its early inception. They duped the people, controlled the medical education system, and government funded health care. Money has great power and with power comes great control. You can't stop it because Profits @ Any Cost control everything. I discovered how the Rockefeller and Carnegie corporations started and funded the modern medical model of health care from watching the docu-series *The Truth About Cancer* and *Quest for the Cures*, produced by Ty and Charlene Bollinger. [36] The Bollinger's had multiple family members die from cancer and decided to conduct their own investigations, and documented their findings.

Ty interviewed G. Edward Griffin author of The Creature from Jekyll Island, a tell all book about the creation, by private bankers, of the Federal Reserve banking system. This is where I learned about the creation and manipulation of the banking system and the medical system, by the

Rockefeller and Carnegie Foundations. [37] This information was another of my red pill moments, and then COVID-19 was introduced, which escalated my awakening.

## Taking the Red Pill liberates you from invisible systems of control

If you didn't know any of the above before, you know now. You have just been elevated past the unconscious incompetence level of learning. You're on the journey to enlightenment and empowerment, but you need an elevated understanding of what we're dealing with. What you need is a different perspective, like a view from a plane or a satellite. Raising your elevation of learning ensures you see more, understand the consequences of not knowing, and learn to master the game of life. We are at an important time in history where it appears 5G is a catalyst for control and ultimate destruction of human kind, if we fail to stop it.

In summary, you've decided to take the red pill, otherwise you wouldn't have gotten this far. You now know why canaries are the alarm system warning people of the dangers of wireless technology, and all forms of man-made EMR. You may have been aware something is not right with the world, which could have come from the covid-19 fiasco, or the rise in infertility, autism, ADD, and ADHD in children, or from realising there's no cure for cancer in the medical system. Understanding why you need to be in control, is the first stage of learning how to actually be in control of your life. Next, you'll gain a greater understanding of what's at stake if nothing changes.

*Mobile (cell) phones are made to be addictive, but rarely do people recognise the power this technology has over the brain.*

# CHAPTER 2
# EVIDENCE OF HARM

*"Challenges are what make life interesting and*
*overcoming them is what makes life meaningful."*

- Joshua J. Marine

## WHERE'S THE EVIDENCE AND WHAT ARE WE EXPOSING HERE?

In my letter to the Greens Political Party MP, I included two scientific reports, detailing the enormous amount of scientific evidence already existing in the scientific community; sufficient to ring alarm bells.

**No. 1.** The Seletun Scientific Statement (SSS) compiled by seven scientists in five countries led by Professor Olle Johansson, of the Karolinska Institute*, Stockholm, Sweden, (*renowned for its contributions to medical research and education), clearly states: **February 3, 2011.**

The scientific journal Reviews on Environmental Health has published a report by scientists of the International Electromagnetic Fields Alliance (IEMFA) calling for greatly reduced exposure limits for electromagnetic radiation from power line and telecommunications technologies, including cell phones and wireless technologies. The statement, called the Seletun Scientific Statement, was written by seven life scientists in five countries, based on a large and growing body of science showing biological effects... **3. Government Actions Are Warranted Now Based on Evidence of Serious Disruption to Biological Systems.**

It can't be much clearer than this Press Release in 2011:

**Karolinska Institute Press Release, Stockholm, Sweden: "Scientists Urge Halt of Wireless Rollout and Call for New Safety Standards: Warning Issued on Risks to Children and Pregnant Women"** [38]

Did you hear about this press release? If the media is meant to present news to the world these concerns should have been addressed by governments in 2011.

**No. 2.** The BioInitiative Report 2012. A Rationale for Biologically-based Exposure Standards for Low-Intensity Electromagnetic Radiation, sums up the issues:

The world's populations – from children to the general public to scientists and physicians – are increasingly faced with great pressures from advertising urging the incorporation of the latest wireless device into their everyday lives. This is occurring even while an elementary understanding of the possible health consequences is beyond the ability of most people to grasp. The exposures are invisible, the testing meters are expensive and technically difficult to operate, the industry promotes new gadgets and generates massive advertising and lobbying campaigns that silence debate, and the reliable, non-wireless alternatives (like wired telephones and utility meters) are being discontinued against public will. There is little labelling, and little or no informed choice.

**In fact, there is often not even the choice to stay with safer, wired solutions, as in the case of the 'smart grid' and smart wireless utility metering, an extreme example of a failed corporate-governmental partnership strategy, apparently for energy conservation.**

If experts are being silenced, the media is controlled and the general population are not aware of the risks to health and the risk to children, we need to find another way to solve the misinformation agenda. The only way to solve this problem is to work together to expose the truth and provide solutions. An alternative education is one of the solutions, and it already exists.

## BUILDING BIOLOGY AND ELECTROBIOLOGY; HOW ELECTRICITY AFFECTS HUMAN BIOLOGY

Building Biology known as Bau-Biologie, originated in Germany in 1970.[39] This is a science that connects the health of the built environment to the health of all life and living things. Building Biologist detect EMF/EMR, toxic mould, chemicals, volatile organic compounds (VOC's) and allergens in buildings and household products, causing chronic disease and ill health. I like to include toxic food as a culprit causing ill-health, but more about that in How to be Smarter than your Smart Phone.

A German doctor, Hubert Palm, found direct correlation between sick buildings and sick people. He called them poisonous houses and when he first detected this phenomenon and alerted designers and architects he was ridiculed by the architectural community. He went on to write The Healthy House, 1968.

Building Biology and Ecology became popular in Europe, because it explained why people were getting sick, hence the term *sick building syndrome*. Building Biology has not gained wide popularity in many countries since its inception 54 years ago, and is rarely mentioned in Australia, especially in the building industry, in hospitals, in cancer care, and in children's services industry. In the USA, Europe, Canada, New Zealand and Australia, contacting a Building Biologist is often the last resort for people when doctors can't help them. Building Biologists identify environmental toxins making people sick and provide solutions based on testing and evidence they find during inspections or consultations. In other words, they identify the cause or issues causing ill-health and help get rid of it.

This brings us to the subject of **Electrobiology**, the study of electricity and biology. Biology is derived from the Greek word bios, and logos means the study of the science of life and living organisms. Electricity produces radiation, detected as a frequency, from electrical wiring and electrical appliances in homes and workplaces and from high voltage transmission lines, substations, electrical transformers and the electrical grid. Electrobiology links biological effects to man-made electricity, often referred to as electromagnetic fields (EMF) but it's much more complex than just a field. George informed me that it's really an electromagnetic force. This is an unseen energy, similar to the energy around a magnet you can detect if you put two magnets together or place metal close to a magnet. Magnetic energy connects or repels, depending on the polarity; defined as the north and south poles. Positive + to negative - attracts, double positive ++ and double negative -- repels.

EMF meters are used to detect EMF in wires and electrical equipment, identified in milligauss (mG) or nano Tesla (nT) or in volts per meter (V/m) by using a gauss meter or EMF meter. Electrobiology also addresses radio waves on the radiofrequency spectrum, including microwaves used in telecommunications. Radio frequency radiation (RFR) broadcast by man-made technology travels at the speed of light. RF transmissions connect to a receiver, like your mobile phone or a wireless modem. We're exposed to much more wireless technology, via telephone transmitters, Wi-Fi and mobile phone communications in the past 30 years, than ever before.

You can't see or hear these waves unless you have a RF meter to detect them. Radiofrequency analysers are the specific meter used to detect EMR/RFR. Professional EMF testing technicians and Building Biologists trained in EMF detection, test for RF using a range of meters because not all meters are created equal. The scientific reading used in Building Biology to test for RF is in microwatts per square meter ($\mu W/m^2$). Radiofrequencies travel much further than EMF from sources of electricity. Electromagnetic energy (EME) from wires or electrical appliances fades as you get further away from the source, over a short distance, depending on power output. Sitting in the near field (500mm) from a fridge or electric heater will test high, while 1.2meters away, or further, may test fine.

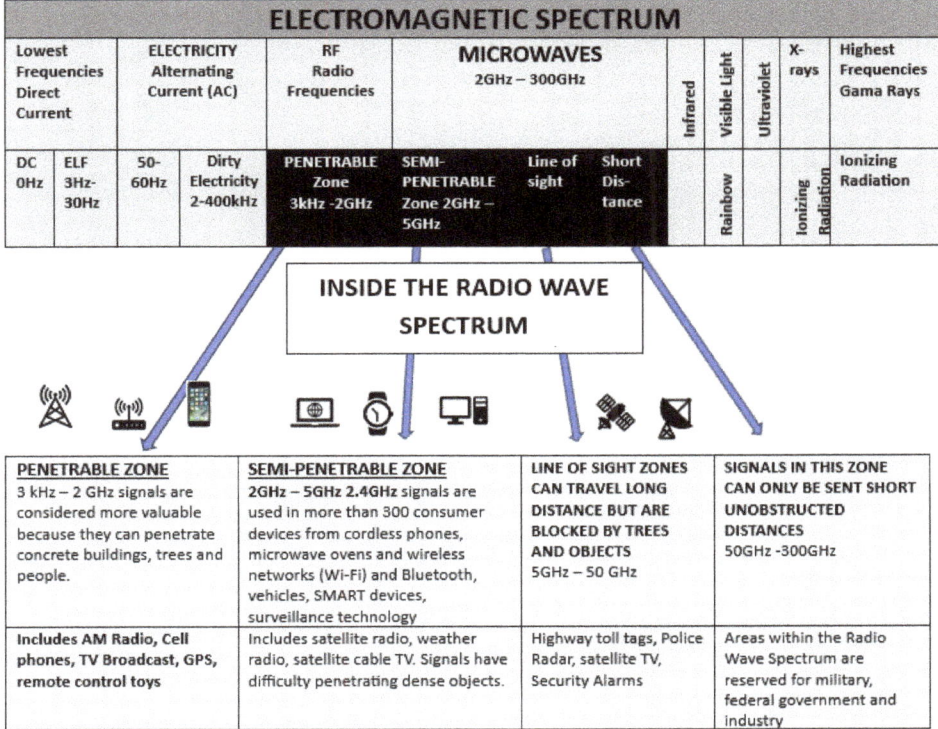

*INSIDE THE RADIO WAVE SPECTRUM*

**The Electromagnetic Spectrum Includes** man-made alternating current (AC) in electrical circuits, electrical equipment, dirty electricity (built environment); AM Radio, FM Radio, TV, Mobile (Cell) phones, Wi-Fi, Satellite Technology, and X-rays and Gama Rays known as ionizing radiation, with sufficient energy to damage DNA instantly

The **Radio Wave Spectrum** sits inside the Electromagnetic Spectrum. All radio waves and frequencies are different lengths depending on the frequency measured in hertz, that travel at the speed of light. One Hertz is one wavelength, which is the distance from wave crest to wave crest and frequency is once cycle per second (more about Hertz shortly).

## Why is the Electromagnetic Spectrum Significant to Biology?

**We are bio-electrical beings:** Our heart and brain produce electric signals to all parts of the body. An electrocardiogram (ECG) records the hearts electrical activity through repeated cardiac cycles. Brain waves are detected by using electroencephalography (EEG). No signal means no life.

As it states in the BioInitiative Report, the stakes are very high. All of life is energy, whether it's biology of living things or plants. Human beings are designed to live in harmony with nature. Biological cells are energy cells containing information and intelligence. Life starts from a single sperm and an egg with built-in intelligence. Fertilization of the egg happens within 24 hours of conception. The fertilized egg rapidly divides evolving into many cells. By week nine of pregnancy the embryo has developed into a foetus. At every stage of development, the body knows what to do, no intervention is needed. This is how intelligent life begins, it's natural. Man-made EMFs can alter or interact with biological processes in the human body at any stage of development and at any age in life.

Scientific evidence proves RF exposures cause damage to health. Children are more susceptible than adults because they have smaller bodies and developing brains. Children do not have any defence mechanisms against wireless technology, and have no say in what they are exposed to. A child's exposure depends on the awareness of their parents, or those that provide early childcare and education.

## Electrical sensitivity (ES) vs electrical hypersensitivity (EHS)

First, I want to establish how and why we are all electrically sensitive. Our brains and body have developed in what's called the Schumann Resonance of 7.83 Hz, known as the heartbeat of the Earth. This is the frequency between Earth and the ionosphere, the upper atmosphere of Earth, approximately 50-400 miles above the Earth's surface, named after the German physicist, Winifred Otto Schumann who discovered it in the 1950's. Lightning activity in the Earth's atmosphere produces energetic waves that fluctuate from 3 Hz up to 60 Hz which are extremely low frequencies (ELF). The scientific community only discovered how important these frequencies are to life when astronauts stationed on a space station became sick. NASA replicated a frequency of 7.83 Hz and solved the problem. Hertz frequencies dictate what goes on in our bodies and our brains.

Our brain functions at different frequencies, depending on what we are doing and what time of day it is. There are five known brainwave states of being:

1.  **Delta waves** < 4 Hz = Deep sleep – Dreamless regeneration and healing

2.  **Theta waves** 4 to 8 Hz = Rapid Eye Movement (REM) sleep. Dreaming state. Deep meditation and access to the unconscious mind

3.  **Alpha waves** 8 to 14 Hz = Relaxation, Creativity, Light meditation and Day dreaming

4.  **Beta waves** 14 to 40 Hz = Concentration, Analytical thinking and Stress and anxiety

5.   **Gamma waves** 40 Hz to 100 Hz = Higher Consciousness. Insight and peak experiences. Higher aspects of cognition

**What is a Hertz (Hz)?** One hertz is the unit of frequency in the International System of Units (SI) describing an electromagnetic wave that travels at the speed of light. Also known as a radio wave. Hertz is named after Heinrich Rudolf Hertz (1857- 1894), the first person to prove existence of electromagnetic waves. For radio waves, a cycle is the distance from wave crest to wave crest, (as indicated on the image below).

1 Hertz = 1 wavelength. One Hertz is one cycle per second

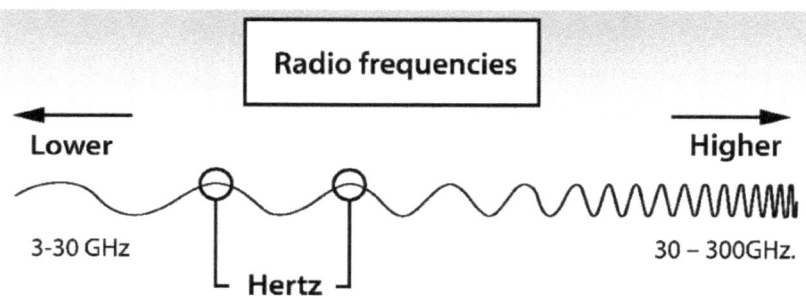

Man-made Hertz frequencies are transmitted by wireless technology, from cell phones, microwave ovens, cordless (DECT) phones (including the base station and handset), wireless networks (Wi-Fi), Bluetooth, highway tolls, police radio, emergency services radios and pagers, GPS and AM radio and TV UHF channels. RF's are broadcast in multiples of Hertz, which are frequencies packed with data. They are pulsed waves, not natural waves.

1 kilohertz (kHz) = 1,000 hertz

1 megahertz (MHz) = 1 million hertz 1,000,000

1 gigahertz (GHz) = 1 billion hertz 1,000,000,000

2.4 GHz (2.4 billion Hertz) is used by more than 300 consumer devices labelled 'SMART' technology. S.M.A.R.T stands for Self-Monitoring, Analysis, and Reporting Technology, used by industry and likely sold to whoever wants to pay for the captured data.

Signals in the 50 GHZ to 300GHz range are mostly reserved for military, federal government and industry.

Brain gamma waves must not be confused with gamma waves on the electromagnetic spectrum. X-rays and gamma waves are ionising radiation, damaging to all life. Ionising radiation is an electromagnetic wave that has sufficient energy to cause damage to DNA as it passes through the body.

X-rays originally called X-radiation are a form of high-energy electromagnetic radiation used in medical imaging. According to Medical News Today, [40] X-rays pose risks and can cause alterations in DNA. They are classed as a carcinogen, which means they should only be used when absolutely necessary. The effects can accumulate in the body and high exposures can have a range of effects from vomiting, bleeding, hair loss and skin damage. This includes all forms of medical imaging from mammograms to ultrasound to CT scans. CT scans take many X-rays as the detector moves around the patient's body. This induces a higher radiation dose than conventional radiography because CT images are reconstructed from many individual X-ray projections (FDA).

Arthur Firstenberg, author of The Invisible Rainbow, [41] [42] a tell all book on the history of electricity, became electrically hypersensitive in his 20's due to X-ray overdose, which ended his medical career. The Invisible Rainbow documents our experiences with electricity and history of major diseases of the industrialised world. Firstenberg identified increases in heart disease, cancer, diabetes and flu epidemics can be correlated to increases in electrical pollution, and specifically increases in radio frequency communications.

Hopefully by now you will have an understanding that man-made electrical energy is not good for your health. It is critical everyone understands exactly what electromagnetic radiation does to the unsuspecting person, child or foetus.

## How Building Biology saved my life

My first encounter with feelings associated with RF radiation from telephone transmission towers and EMF pollution, happened when we were living in Richmond, close to the central business district of Melbourne, Australia. I had recently started my consulting business and was conducting EMF assessments for clients locally. I had wired all computers and a printer through a switch box (multi-port device) with Ethernet cabling from a modem. I used a wired internet connection, and data cabling to ensure I could turn all Wi-Fi off. I tested it and thought I was safe, until I started experiencing body aches and pains and often felt pain in my back, neck and shoulders, sometimes quite intense.

Living in Queensland, prior to moving to Melbourne, I'd focused on health and fitness as a priority. I had monthly visits to a chiropractor, had consulted with a Naturopath to make sure I was on the right track and followed a daily fitness regime. In my early thirties I'd trained as a fitness leader with the Institute of Fitness, through the Launceston University. For most of my thirties I took ten aerobic classes a week, one each morning and one in the evenings. I knew what being fit and healthy felt like. In my fifties, living in Melbourne, my aim was to continue to stay active and find another chiropractor to keep my body in tip top condition.

Unfortunately, my new chiropractor wanted a full body X-ray to assess my spine. This was a gigantic mistake. During the two X-rays I could feel the radiation, which had never happened before and my body ached for days afterwards. I continued seeing the chiropractor for a few weeks but I felt worse, not better. I decided to take RF readings in our apartment, and was shocked to find the RF in the bedroom was extreme, in what I call the danger zone; well above a safe level based on Building Biology guidelines. From that moment on we slept with a shielding canopy over the bed. I needed to recover at night from the daily radiation exposure in the built environment. The shielding canopy protected me at night from RF coming from telephone towers within one kilometre of our building.

Our bodies are designed to heal naturally and one of the miracles of life is the power of the pineal gland located in the centre of the brain. This gland plays a vital role at night by regulating our circadian rhythm and secreting melatonin. Melatonin works as a powerful antioxidant in the prevention of cancer and other diseases. If you're exposed to wireless radiation at night your pineal gland detects the frequencies as light waves and fails to release melatonin. When this happens, you wake but do not feel refreshed. I could feel the negative effects in my body. If it wasn't for Building Biology training, I would not have recognised the cause of my symptoms.

When our lease ran out in January 2018, we decided to move to a townhouse in Port Melbourne, near Port Phillip Bay, which had fairly low readings of around 16 $\mu W/m^2$. For sensitive people anything over 1 $\mu W/m^2$ is a concern but at that stage I didn't believe I was electrically hypersensitive because I was functioning quite well, so I assumed the location would be fine.

All was good for about eighteen months. We were swimming in the bay and taking long walks every weekend of 10-15 kilometres. We loved our frequent walks to the Botanic Gardens and explored much of the area without using our car. Eleven months later we were forced to move because the owners of the townhouse wanted to move in, so chose another town house in the same block about 25 metres up the street. In April 2019 my health deteriorated, my fitness dropped off and my body ached and I couldn't sleep so I took RF readings and was astounded; the radio frequency radiation had jumped to 2,500 $\mu W/m^2$ which is classified as extreme or what's called an extreme anomaly, compared to natural background radiation. Anything over 1,000 $\mu W/m^2$ is known to cause health effects. We immediately installed the shielding canopy over the bed.

Shielding fabric is made of copper wire coated in cotton that blocks radio frequencies, but does not eliminate electromagnetic fields from electrical wiring or appliances. Inside the canopy I was safe. The RF reading was 0.5 $\mu W/m^2$ which meant I had a safe place to sleep. I shielded my office with aluminium wall wrap, earthed with copper wire to a stake in the ground outside the window, and my computer was connected to a wired internet connection. No wireless technology was allowed inside the home and no electrical lights or radio/alarm clocks next to the bed. Everything was tested to ensure it was safe.

The trouble is you can't live 100% of your time in a shielded environment if you want to have a normal life. I continued to provide services to clients and travelled all over the country, wherever people needed me to conduct EMF testing and mould inspections. In between I worked from my home office on healthy home consults and continued to learn more about 5G and how to reduce EMF exposure.

Interestingly, it was in April 2019 when the National Broadband Network (NBN) was rolled out in Port Melbourne. NBN is a government initiative to upgrade connections to the internet using fibreoptics, supposed to be a superior high performance data communications network, replacing the slower old copper wire telephone connections. We stuck with our ADSL copper wire because the fibre option was not available to us. What seemed to be happening was an explosion of wireless technology and an increase in transmitters placed on light poles, power poles and existing telephone communication towers. Telecommunications companies promoted wireless connections, mainly because Wi-Fi was easier and cheaper than opting for a fibre upgrade. Not all fibre connections worked as well as they should. Old copper wires owned by Telstra (formerly Telecom Australia), were being phased out. In many locations they no longer service properties connected to copper wire. Copper wire was originally used for telephones and then Broadband internet connections.

During 2019 I started to lose function so much so I could hardly walk to the beach anymore and when I did it would take me days to recover. I had literally become sensitive to the environment and couldn't stop the attack on my body.

We moved again, out of the city into the Eastern suburbs, where we found a place connected to NBN, with Ethernet cabling throughout the house and a swimming pool, an added bonus. RF readings in the home were very low. My only concern was the solar panels connected to an inverter, known to introduce electromagnetic interference (EMI) on the wiring of the house. EMI is mostly referred to as dirty electricity (DE). EMI also comes from switch mode power devices that change direct current (DC) to alternating current (AC). Devices such as mobile phones, iPads, laptops/notebooks, and smart watches work on battery power that needs to be recharged by plugging into an AC power point. EMI is also emitted from appliances with variable power options, such as electric fans, dimmer switches, LED lighting and of course solar inverters, which turn the DC from the solar panels into AC used in home appliances. Knowing this, we turned off the breaker switch to our bedroom every night and continued to sleep under the shielding canopy.

My health was slightly better and then corona virus was announced worldwide. This is where my story gains a greater level of understanding. I received an email from Dr. Bruce Lipton, [43] a cell biologist from USA and author of Biology of Belief. I had booked to do a PSYCH-K course in Tao, New Mexico in August 2020. In his email he said *"don't worry about the corona virus because it's only the regular flu that comes around each year."* During this time a lot of people were stopped from conducting their business, me included.

Luckily my husband's job in construction was safe at the time, enabling him to earn an income. This provided me an opportunity to do more training and research. I attended multiple EMF and 5G summits, medical conferences and read more research and books on EMF and 5G to gain a better understanding of electrical hypersensitivity.

Once again, in this house my health deteriorated. I was experiencing symptoms similar to multiple sclerosis (MS). Loss of function, chronic fatigue, muscle pain, I had problems walking, I would lose my balance and be unsteady even when walking on level ground. My legs felt weak and I could barely walk 100m without feeling exhausted. It was so unusual for me to feel this way and I knew at this stage EMR/EMF was having an enormous effect biologically. If it wasn't for Building Biology I would have gone to a doctor and been diagnosed with MS or something similar. Instead, we moved to the country, on 20 acres where we're surrounded by trees and no telephone transmission towers in sight.

We created a safe environment in a shed where the RF readings are 0.05 $\mu W/m^2$. No one is allowed in my safe space with a mobile phone turned on. If anyone comes in, I feel it immediately and get them to turn it off. My body has recovered somewhat, but not to its full potential. I continue my search to find solutions and undertake the odd Building Biology consult.

Trouble is we are not permitted to live in the shed, according to our local Council/Shire authorities, because it is not a Class 1 building, suitable for habitation, even though we've made it as safe as possible with low VOC products, (VOC stands for volatile organic compounds), timber flooring, double glazed windows, thermal and acoustic insulation and we've installed shielded cabling on all electrical outlets and Ethernet cabling to a modem that's connected to the NBN via a fixed wireless transmitter/receiver 50m up the hill from the shed, located on another building, and cabled underground to our shed. I use a wired telephone handset connected to a modem with voice over internet protocol (VoIP), that's safe. Location and distance from telephone towers is extremely important, as is a natural environment, to enable you to heal.

Today, in April 2025, I feel 80% better than I did three years ago. No MS symptoms or chronic fatigue unless I'm exposed to mobile phones or venture back into the modern world where wireless radiation is prolific. Much of my body has healed but my reaction to all forms of EMF keeps me confined to my home and locked away from connecting to people that have no idea there is a global health crisis caused by wireless technology.

## How do human bodies and electromagnetic radiation collide?

Dr Andrew Goldsworthy,[44] a retired lecturer from Imperial College London, explained how calcium metabolism works in living cells and how cells, tissue and organisms are affected by electrical and electromagnetic fields, In the article titled; The Cell Phone and the Cell – the Role of Calcium; he explained how weak electromagnetic fields from Wi-Fi, cordless phones, and cell phones produce serious health effects. EMF causes damage to glands, resulting in obesity and related disorders, chronic fatigue, autism, multiple chemical sensitivity, increases allergies and early dementia, loss of fertility, DNA damage and cancer.

Man-made EMR generates alternating electric currents that flow through cells and tissues and remove structurally-important calcium ions from cell membranes, which makes them leak. This is similar to the theory Professor Martin Pall, from Washington State University, uses when he suggests electromagnetic radiation has a direct effect on the Voltage-Gated Calcium Channel of cells, causing an increase of nitic oxide synthesis. The nitic oxide diffuses out of the cells causing an increase of intracellular calcium (Ca2+).

Professor Martin Pall wrote a Review titled 5G: Great risk for EU, U.S. and International Health! [45]

## Compelling Evidence for Eight Distinct Types of Great Harm Caused by Electromagnetic Field (EMF) Exposures and the Mechanism that Causes Them.

In the review (a compilation of many research studies) Martin Pall provides a high level of scientific certainty, and evidence of harm caused by microwave frequency EMF exposures.

**How EMF harms our body:**

1. EMR/RFR attacks our nervous system, causing neurological effects (brain inflammation, emotional effects and reduced function).

2. Frequencies attack our hormonal systems, needed for reproduction. No reproduction means no children.

3. Causes oxidative stress and free radical damage, contributing to all chronic diseases.

4. Affects DNA, causing single strand and double strand breaks, producing mutations in future generations.

5. Increases levels of apoptosis (programmed cell death), specifically important because cell death causes both neurodegenerative diseases (destruction of the nervous system, particularly the brain) and infertility.

6. Causes lower male and female fertility, lower libido and increased levels of spontaneous abortion.

7. Produces excessive intracellular calcium and excessive calcium signalling, causing health effects, damage to glands, obesity, autism, MCS, increases in allergies and early dementia, damages DNA, as detailed by Dr Andrew Goldsworthy.

8. Contributes to 15 different mechanisms in cells of our bodies, ultimately causing cancer.

Martin Pall stated there is substantial evidence that EMFs cause life threatening cardiac effects, contribute to very early onset dementias, including Alzheimer's, and EMF exposures during pregnancy and shortly after birth can cause ADHD and autism.

EMF levels in today's world are **7.2 million times too high.** Sensitivity to EMF is predicted by the laws of physics (natural philosophy). Therefore, the physics and the biology are each pointing to the same mechanism of harm. 5th Generation technology is designed to destroy lives, and as Professor Martin Pall says,

"it's insanity to continue to roll out more 5G and 6G technology."

## Health effects are direct effects of man-made frequencies

For anyone not understanding the EMF effect, let me explain a little about biology and what makes your body function as it is meant to. Each cell in your body is like a mini battery pack of energy, holding voltage, and according to Dr Bruce Lipton, a cell biologist, the average membrane potential of a cell is 70 millivolts or .07 volts. [46] We have 70 trillion cells that work together in collaboration with one another sending signals to other cells and organs to respond. That's what cells do, because they have a brain, that's why cell walls are called membranes. Our innate intelligence and every system in our body works via electric signals from our brain, our heart, our gut and our skin and everything in between. Nothing works in isolation and nothing works properly if the signals don't connect or, if they are damaged and don't get a chance to repair.

When you leave a Wi-Fi modem on at night, or your phone is on the bedside table being used as an alarm clock, or worse under your pillow, your brain detects the transmissions and your pineal gland doesn't secrete melatonin, the antioxidant needed to repair cells, resulting in sleeplessness (insomnia), lethargy, chronic fatigue, memory problems etc., causing your biological systems to break down over time.

Wireless technology interferes with the gut microbiome, which consists of more bacteria than cells in the body. Good gut bacteria are needed to stay healthy. Wireless technology disrupts the natural process of the immune system, hindering the process of repairing and rejuvenating cells. We have different systems that keep us alive, all connected to our central nervous system, called our autonomic nervous system, meaning you don't have to tell it what to do, it knows.

There are two modes to our autonomic nervous system. Our parasympathetic nervous system is our rest and repair system responsible for rejuvenation and recovery and our sympathetic nervous system, is our "fight or flight" response to save us when we're in danger. They primarily work unconsciously to regulate many systems in our body. When you're in "flight or fight" mode the body is prepped to run away or stand and fight, and blood is automatically transferred to areas of the body to meet physical demand, along with adrenalin to help you run away, so the tiger doesn't eat you for lunch. The problem these days, it's not usually a tiger, it's your boss or the financial burden you're under or it's an invisible energy field you can't see but your body can detect. **Invisible RF radiation puts your body under stress, and enacts the "fight or fight" process.**

## Reactions to EMR/RFR are early signs of EHS

One day on a tram in Melbourne, packed with people on mobile phones my heart raced, my head hurt, I felt nauseous and I had this almighty sense to get the hell out of the tram. Some people might call that feeling anxiety, but I knew it was RF radiation overload. That was at the beginning of my EHS activation in 2018.

The two modes of the autonomic nervous system do not function at the same time. It's either one or the other, depending on your situation. If you're in the "fight or fight" mode all the time because you live with stress or radiation that never goes away, your body doesn't get the chance to repair, and you become sick. It's actually forcing you to do something to save your life, but you can't get away from an invisible tiger. This means your body never gets a chance to initiate the parasympathetic nervous system, designed to repair and rejuvenate the body during rest and relaxation. I hope you're joining the dots like I've done, and realise the rise and rise of autoimmune diseases/disorders is linked to the rise and rollout of wireless/microwave radiation in the environment.

Collecting evidence is how a good detective works. A detective aims to find the culprit causing harm or trying to kill you. RFR is the culprit and what appears to be happening is the increasing release of technology, slowly over time, has an effect labelled as something else, like an autoimmune disease, heart disease, stroke, MS or a neurological condition. Microwave radiation is designed to make people sick, with the intention of making money via the pharmaceutical backed medical system.

# AUTOIMMUNE DISEASE; WHAT THEY ARE NOT TELLING YOU

I refer here, to a research paper by Dr. Miller stating "both autoimmunity and autoimmune diseases are dramatically increasing in many parts of the world, likely as a result of changes in our exposures to environmental factors." [47]

> **"Current evidence implicates the momentous alterations in our food, xenobiotics, air pollution, infections, personal lifestyles, stress, and climate change as causes for these increases."**

Dr. Miller goes on to say, there is a need to understand autoimmune disease risk factors and pathogeneses and improve therapeutic, diagnostic and prevention approaches. He mentions that the cost of inaction will be immense.

That's code for, they will make lots and lots of money out of autoimmune disease and have to do more research on this autoimmunity problem.

Autoimmunity is defined as self-reactive components of the adaptive immune system, which cause clinically apparent pathology in the case of autoimmune diseases.

I'm gathering, self-reactive, means it is brought on by the body. It may be, but what's the cause? Natural intelligence in the past did not create autoimmune disease.

I'm very cynical; I doubt they will find the cause because they are looking in the wrong place. Autoimmune diseases (disorders) are not caused by something inside the body; they are caused by something outside the body. And I'm not referring to climate change, which Dr. Miller mentions, I'm referring to the rise and rise of electromagnetic radiation that's known to cause a multitude of biological harm, and the ever-increasing chemical load the body has to endure. We'll cover chemicals in How to be Smarter than Your Smart Phone.

**Not once** in the article did Dr. Miller suggest that the rise in wireless technology and 5G millimetre waves to more and more locations worldwide, have any link, let alone a direct effect on the increase in autoimmune diseases.

Here's a list of some of the diseases he is referring to:

Type 1 Diabetes

All inflammatory bowel disease

Celiac disease

Psoriasis

Ulcerative colitis

Multiple sclerosis

Chron's disease

Rheumatoid arthritis

Systemic lupus

Behcet's disease

Systemic sclerosis

Myositis

I'll throw in a few more listed on Healthline:

Addison's disease

Graves' disease

Sjögrens disease

Hashimoto's thyroiditis

Myasthenia gravis

Autoimmune vasculitis

Pernicious anaemia

There are over 80 different types of autoimmune disorders. Wikipedia says the cause is largely unknown. Of course they'd say that; this is the system they use to misinform the public. Wikipedia is a master of deception.

What do autoimmune disorders have in common? In the early stages, the symptoms are very similar. They include; fatigue, muscle aches, swelling, dizziness or light headedness. Most of the diseases/disorders on the list include symptoms of weakness, headaches; the immune system attacks the blood vessels, hair loss, weight gain, weight loss; the disorder attacks the glands, your joints, eyes and skin. Swelling of the thyroid gland, rapid heart rate, numbness and balance issues. It effects your eyes, heart, kidneys and nerves. Does the body really attack itself? Or is there an invisible beast causing damage to cells, they are not identifying?

This list of symptoms is nearly exactly the same as George's and my reactions to all forms of electromagnetic radiation, yet EMR or EMF is not listed in Dr. Millers paper. I wonder why? Is anyone smelling something profitable?

My belief is that autoimmune diseases are a direct effect of environmental exposures and likely EMF is a trigger, or contributor to a synergistic effect. It is not my opinion alone. Both Dr. Sam Milham, author of *Dirty Electricity*; *Electrification and the Diseases of Civilization* [48], and Arthur Firstenberg, author of *The Invisible Rainbow,* investigated the history of EMF/RFR and both present similar ideas i.e. that the cause of disease is EMF, and many more experts dealing with health effects report similar findings.

> Dr. Milham warns that because of the recent proliferation of radio frequency radiation from cell phones and towers, terrestrial antennas, Wi-Fi and Wi-max systems, broadband internet over power lines, and personal electronic equipment, we may be facing a looming epidemic of morbidity and mortality. He exposes how electricity is causing our current epidemics of asthma, diabetes and obesity.

In a webinar on 5G-An Undeniable Risk, by Dr Sharon Goldberg [49], a medical doctor in the USA, who's a campaigner for safe levels of RFR, provided a presentation at an EMF Summit highlighting the facts. I made note of these issues.

- Radiofrequency EMF (RF-EMF) exposure is scientifically proven to cause harm to all life forms.

- Oxidative stress is a key mechanism of harm

- Human harm from RF-EMF is common, but often misdiagnosed

Jeff Barlow posted a video on YouTube of the presentation to Congress by Dr. Sharon Goldberg. [50] What's even more interesting are the comments below in the chat. I've captured one comment for you to read, which highlights my concern.

> About 6 years ago for my job I had to regularly test an app we were developing on 6x Wi-Fi enabled iPads, 2x smartphones, a smart watch and 2x PCs (also surrounded by 15 other pcs/macs). After 3 weeks of periodically using the devices, I became unbelievably ill, with manic depression, neurological issues, brain fog, problems speaking, aches and pains in my body, my blood felt like treacle and unbelievable fatigue. When i took time off work I got better, returned to work to do my usual tasks but when I revisited the app testing with multi devices the illness came back. Trying to talk about EMF sensitivity to people is very difficult, they think you are crazy, odd or just trying to avoid doing a task. Now with the plans to roll out 5G in my area I am starting to get very VERY concerned. [40 see comments]

## Getting to the Truth

I wish to shed light on what I learned from David Icke, an ex-UK footballer, turned investigator and author of multiple books and long-time activist, who's been exposing, to the world, how the Profits @ Any Cost, use PROBLEM – REACTION – SOLUTION methodology to control, steal, plunder and profit from humanity. It's been happening all over the world for a very long time.[51]

They, (mechanisms of control, called the Deep State (DS)) create a problem, unbeknown to the general public, it then causes a reaction they highlight in the media - medical – banking - political - war industry. Then, they come up with a solution, that makes them a lot of money and/or enables control of the masses. This is a multi-faceted system used for many years. David is one of many that exposed the 9/11 take-down of the twin towers, which was an organised controlled demolition. Architects and Engineers for 9/11 Truth, state that World Trade Center 7 was destroyed by an implosion, causing it to freefall into its own footprint. [52] Watching the videos on ae911truth.org is a must, to learn how they got away with murder, fraud and psychological warfare. AI generated videos instigated by the DS and broadcast through the mainstream media worldwide, told the story they wanted you to believe. I remember watching the news feed, and could hardly believe my eyes. At the time I did not doubt the story, but later when evidence appeared on alternative media, it was easy to see the fakery, and I realised I'd been tricked like everyone else. I have watched controlled demolitions in the past, so understood completely what was being shown on TV was not caused by a plane. This is backed up by American Architects and Engineers, that design buildings this size.

They used the PROBLEM – REACTION - SOLUTION system to reduce gun ownership in Australia, after the Port Arthur massacre on April 28, 1996. I was living in Tasmania at the time, when Martin Bryant, a lone intellectually impaired gunman apparently shot and killed 35 people during a raging rampage. I had no idea it was a covert operation to disarm the Australian people. It was only when I delved into our legal rights on the website Know Your Rights Group[53], that I discovered it was a total fabrication, likely instigated by the CIA.[54] It was George that convinced me Martin Bryant was innocent. When he heard the gunshots on the TV coverage, he said that's not an intellectually disabled person, that's a trained sharp shooter. Until I was privileged to receive an alternative education, I had no idea the Port Arthur massacre was contrived. Innocent people died and I doubt, the truth will come out publicly, because those in control, would do all in their power to stop these crimes becoming common knowledge.

Why do I believe what I believe, I hear your ask. The fact is I didn't believe in conspiracy theories, or doubt the mainstream news until I had firsthand experience of being lied to, and discovered how the media and government hide the truth. I was a Dr Karl fan and previously never doubted him. Dr Karl Kruszelnicki is a prominent science communicator, providing answers to listener's questions on his ABC Radio talkback show. The Australian Broadcasting Commission (ABC) is a government funded TV and Radio station. I was alerted to his response when he was asked about 5G technology; he stated there was no cause for concern and that 5G was safe. I immediately contacted the ABC, via Facebook, and was told they did not want to know what I had to share about the science of radiofrequencies or the harm caused by wireless technology. I was quickly dismissed and told my information was not wanted. I posted my thoughts on Facebook and they were taken down.

How many times do you need to be alerted to corruption at the highest level to realise the truth is not being told. It's not just 5G technology, and the harm it causes, I believe every environmental toxin is manufactured to cause harm and/or to make Profits @ Any Cost rich. The same systems of harm were instigated by cigarettes, the spraying of DDT, lead in petrol, asbestos in manufactured products, (specifically building products), causing enormous harm worldwide, and it took decades to gradually phase out the use of it in manufacturing. EPA. [55]

> "There are two ways to be fooled. One is to believe what isn't true; the other is to refuse to believe what is true."

~Soren Kierkegaard, Danish philosopher, 1813 – 1855

A standard education is controlled by money, intended outcomes and a narrative designed to brainwash people with fake science and misinformation. They pervert the course of justice, including the truth about wireless technology. They manipulate using AI and never expose who the puppet masters are. It's impossible to source truth from controlled main stream media TV channels or news publications. It's necessary to delve deeper to detect the truth, or search for people, like me, who question what they are being told by doctors, educators or government agencies and politicians. You really can't believe what you hear on TV or read in a newspaper.

After the covid conundrum I started to read more stories and books exposing how the Deep State actually operated. This is a secret group within government, government agencies and organisations all around the world. I found this topic hard to believe until I read *Behold a Pale Horse* by William (Bill) Cooper. [56] Bill was a former Unites States Naval Intelligence Briefing Team member. He accidently became involved with those that held power within the secret government groups. His intent was to transform beliefs and empower audiences with information he sourced from government documents, which he revealed in his book. He unveiled the truth about the war on drugs, the Secret Government and UFOs. He discovered the CIA (Central Intelligence agency) was the instigator of crimes, unbeknown to the people. Well worth reading to gain insights into how they pulled off crimes of gigantic proportions. Bill identified how a group of elite power-hungry individuals, under the umbrella of the New World Order plan to control individual behaviour and may establish electronic or chemical implants, creating a world where no one will be allowed to have a child without permission. They have a plan to take over world governments and control humanity with a One World Government. It's fascinating how this situation is very fluid (moving in different directions) at the moment, due to many people becoming aware of a movement to take back power by a group of good military leaders often referred to as Q. I'm not privy to what their plan is and rely on others to keep me informed. I will provide links on wellintent.net for those that wish to learn more or want to do their own research, which is the only way to become an enlightened individual.

Let's get back to reality for now; to understand what we're dealing with, and what the world needs, which is knowing what to do and who to trust. I'd like to share some consults to create an image in your mind of the reality in this day and age. Names have been changed for privacy and protection.

## Building Biology consults reveal the living truth

One of my first consults was for an older couple, in their sixties, who'd moved into a new house three months earlier, in a relatively new subdivision in a country town in Victoria. Both were quite unwell. Betty, had been diagnosed with Parkinsons disease 20 years earlier and coped quite well on medication to slow down the disease, even running a business, until they moved into their new home. Since moving, Betty's health deteriorated dramatically and her body was failing to function. It was her daughter that contacted me – she was concerned the new home was making her sick.

As soon as I arrived, I could feel the negative energy and asked if they could turn off all wireless devices in the home, including their wireless modem and mobile phones. RF readings were very high and when I walked into the room Betty used as her work room, the readings went sky high. Outside the window I could see a telephone transmission tower. I'd found the biggest cause of their problems.

*Telephone transmitters (masts) are now everywhere in the landscape, and hard to dodge.*

My advice was to move. Asking to have the tower removed was not an option in my experience, so moving house was the most practical solution. I didn't mention shielding because shielding is very complicated and it can go horribly wrong if not completed appropriately and tested with EMF and RF meters to ensure the environment is safe. Occupants and visitors would need to be educated to turn off all devices in a shielded home. No wireless technology, watches, tablets, phones etc can be taken into a shielded room or home, and definitely not used, because wireless tech creates a microwave oven effect. With a phone tower this close, spending time outside, using their BBQ area, which they loved, would cause detrimental health effects, and I didn't believe this situation was fixable.

Betty asked me to take readings at their rural property 17 kilometres away, where they'd lived prior to moving. When I got there the environment felt good. I have a sense of calmness in my body when I'm in a natural environment, and the country property proved to be in a perfect location. Readings outside were no more than 5.0 $\mu W/m^2$ and inside was even better at 0.5 $\mu W/m^2$ and perfect for recovery. I suggested returning to this property until they found a more suitable home in a safer location. When I rang twelve months later to see how they were getting on, they had not taken my advice to move, instead Betty's husband had the home painted with shielding paint. They were extremely unwell and not happy. For some reason they couldn't shift their thinking, and relocate. I have found this to be a common theme. We'll discuss shifting your thinking, in How the Mind Works.

**An unintended consult with a good result:** Sasha, a lady I was dealing with regarding financial matters, asked me for some motherly advice about her son. He was not sleeping and had recently started having night terrors; waking up screaming in the middle of the night. Her son Ashley was three years old, and they had no family in Australia. I suggested I was not a normal mum and I might be able to help if she wanted to work with me. It was a phone consult, not a house inspection, because covid lockdowns were in place. Often, I can do an investigation by phone sufficiently enough to help people in trouble. When I asked her about her home environment, she advised they were both working from home. Her husband was an accountant and they had computers connected via Wi-Fi to a wireless modem. Recently they had built a new home with SMART technology and installed smart devices, like video surveillance, smart lighting, smart window blinds, all wirelessly connected to a smart panel on the wall, and operable from a mobile phone. Every evening after work they were going to the new house to paint the interior, and took their son with them. It was after these visits Ashley started having night terrors. Sasha had taken him to a doctor, who said Ashley would grow out of it and there was nothing he could do.

Alarm bells were ringing, and I suggested they turn off all wireless technology, including their mobile phones, unless they needed to use them, install a landline or VoIP phone, and use Ethernet cables directly connected to their computers from their modem/router. I emailed some scientific research and gave her a link to my blog, *How to be Smarter Than Your Smart Phone*, which included instructions to reduce wireless exposure and I explained why smart technology was not really smart. You'll learn more about smart tech in Chapter 3.

A couple of days later Sasha phoned to let me know Ashley had slept through the night for the first time in his life and she was very grateful. Thankfully, they were going to follow my instructions going forward.

It may appear that children are often affected but parents are not. I believe it is much more complex. Yes, children have smaller bodies and may be influenced by EMF in different ways to adults. If you look for evidence it's not hard to find. The BioInitiative Report has extensive scientific evidence, but weirdly, they always say, they need to do more research. Stories I've provided make it obvious more scientific research will not solve the problem, and expecting it to change outcomes is, in my opinion part of the problem. We need action NOW, not next year, or in five years' time. The cost of doing nothing is incomprehensible. It could mean the end of intelligent life on Earth as we know it, if nothing changes.

Another consult for a couple with two children identified multiple environmental issues. Their son was diagnosed on the autism spectrum at six years old and their health practitioner advised them to consult a Building Biologist to have their home tested. Their son had been fine up to the age of five and they thought mould may be the problem and they were correct, because walls around two chimneys, one in the boy's bedroom and the other in the daughter's room at the front of the house were wet, when tested with a moisture meter. Wet materials are evidence of mould. Where there's moisture, there is mould. I didn't believe testing with a bio-pump to capture air particulates and genre of mould would help, when fixing the water leaks and removing the wet materials was the highest priority to solve the mould problem. This wasn't an insurance claim after storm damage, therefore spending money on testing and paying for a report would not be beneficial, when they needed to spend money on remediation. What I did identify was four electrical items causing concern. The boy slept in a bedroom with a solar inverter on the outside wall, next to his bed. He was exposed to dirty electricity (EMI) from the inverter, and a smart meter, emitting RFR 24/7 was on another exterior wall. In the home office next door was a Wi-Fi modem and in his sister's room across the hallway was a Google Home Mini, all emitting high levels of wireless radiation. The boy was surrounded and exposed to high levels of RFR and the parents had no idea it was dangerous. Fortunately, they had created a new living area at the back of the home and had wired Ethernet cable to the smart TV. This is an example of what can happen when you don't know what you don't know.

## EHS STORIES THAT MAKE YOU CRY

George and I discussed some of the most disturbing cases, where people have committed suicide because the systems failed to save them. Some of the most harrowing stories I've heard come from parents with children that are electrically sensitive. I know of people in Australia, UK, USA and Canada. One example is Charlene Acres from Ottawa, Canada, who has a daughter that struggles to attend school because her EHS is so bad. The school system does not accommodate children with EHS, leaving them with no options. EHS causes social, mental and physical hardship yet schools fail in their duty of care. You can hear her story on YouTube. [57]

In July 2018, Nick Pineault, The EMF Guy from Canada, (a proactive journalist and educator about all things EMF), interviewed Maria August who suffers from EHS.[58] Maria shared her story with Nick, on his YouTube channel, talking about the difficulties she experienced. The onset of her EHS seemed to coincide with a traumatic car accident. Her symptoms were getting worse and it wasn't clear why, until she realised the place where she was recovering was next to a bank of 16 smart meters on the outside wall. Smart meters emit microwave radiation by sending signals back to the electricity company intermittently 24/7. Over time her symptoms became so extreme she could not venture outside; fluorescent lights, vehicles, and all Wi-Fi signals caused her to become extremely ill. Maria, like a lot of other EHS people are not catered for in society. EHS people often become homeless, living in vehicles, tents and even caves. Her situation became so bad she took her own life; in the hope it would send a message to others that EHS people need help.

> Nick mentioned *"it is ludicrous and a crime against humanity that EHS people are ignored and often shunned by others because they don't understand."*

## Have people gone crazy due to technology or lost their minds?

George told me of his latest trip to hospital, that turned into a nightmare. He needed some treatment and didn't have another option. He took his shielding material with him to keep him covered while in hospital and asked all nurses and staff to not come into his room with mobile phones, and not to wear their smart watches. They took no notice and he would ask them to leave. In the end no one came in to check on him because being connected to their technology was more important than looking after a patient. He declared he would never visit a hospital again.

I recommend watching Electrosensitivity: Tortured by Technology? (Short Documentary) ¦ BBC Stories, on YouTube [59]

# EHS SYMPTOMS; UNDERSTANDING BIOLOGICAL EFFECTS

Constant exposure to electromagnetic force can produce symptoms often diagnosed as inflammatory conditions, like autoimmune diseases and/or chronic illnesses with no remedy. Here's a thought; could feeling old be a sign of Electrical Sensitivity? Absolutely.

**FACT:** EMF expert Dr. Magda Havas states *"exposure to EMF has a rapid aging effect on the body."* That means anyone feeling a little bit aged and weary, might like to do some research or some testing. [60] [61] Getting rid of wireless technology could be the best anti-aging strategy ever invented, here's why.

**Symptoms** often associated with EHS include:

> headaches,
>
> sleep disturbances and insomnia,
>
> lethargy,
>
> fibromyalgia,
>
> muscle and joint pain,
>
> thrombosis effects (clotting or clumping of blood cells),
>
> chronic fatigue,
>
> depression,
>
> anxiety,
>
> redness or burning of the skin or hands when using mobile devices.

**Symptoms listed in Michael Bevington's book on Electromagnetic Sensitivity include:**

> chest pain,
>
> heart arrhythmias,
>
> cold extremities, especially in the hands and feet,

burning sensations in the feet or legs,

concentration and memory problems,

cardiac palpitations,

high or low blood pressure,

nosebleeds,

shortness of breath,

coughs,

irratibility,

difficulty learning, irritability and hyperactivity especially in children,

lack of concentration,

short or long-term memory impairment,

dry skin,

crawling sensations on the skin

restless legs,

facial flushing,

growths or lumps on the skin,

altered appetite,

digestive problems,

flatulence,

food intolerances.

Eyes and sight can be affected. Impaired vision, smarting dry eyes, pressure behind the eyes, pain or a gritty feeling, eyelid tremors or tics.

## Other physiological conditions include:

abnormal menstruation,

brittle nails,

hair loss,

itchy scalp,

metal redistribution,

thirst / dryness of lips, tongue and mouth, and

incontinence.

**EHS increases** allergies, chemical sensitivity, light sensitivity, noise sensitivity, and smell sensitivity (ES-UK). [62]

Scientific research indicates that EMF and RFR affects the cardiovascular system, cognitive function, neurological function and your emotional state of mind. The musculoskeletal and respiratory systems are both affected, and EMF affects your brain and heart, leading to Alzheimers, dementia, heart attack and stroke. This is why we must take long term exposure very seriously.

THAT'S A BIG LIST OF SYMPTOMS. No wonder Profits @ any Cost don't want you to know about EMF/RFR.

How many symptoms do you have?

Do you know of others with symptoms that could benefit from a better education?

## Recognised biological effects of EMF/EMR exposure and variable reactions

Even though I was trained to detect all forms of EMF, I failed to comprehend what was happening to me in the early stages of electrical sensitivity and didn't take the symptoms as seriously as I should have. If I'd understood the repercussions I would have acted sooner, rather than later. That's why I've included this list of variables to help others recognise any or all the health effects caused by EMF exposure listed above.

**Bio-Accummulation:**

Bio-accumulation occurs with cumulative exposures over time. This happens similar to accumulating interest on interest, known as compounding interest, where the effects are greater the greater the exposure. EMR/RFR accumulates in the body causing more or greater effects. Cumulative exposures can produce an increase in symptoms, making symptoms from chronic (long-term/constant) exposure more difficult to recognise than from acute (short-term) exposure.

**Delay in Symptoms:**

Symptoms vary from person to person and symptoms can be delayed after an acute exposure for a few hours or even days. Often the more sensitive a person becomes, the more variable the symptoms or the more they may change.

**Diurnal (daytime) state:**

Symptoms vary according to daytime activity. A person's own internal electromagnetic field often declines during the day.

**Continuance or persistence of symptoms:**

Individual symptoms may vary over time. Symptoms can last for a short or a long time or they may become worse. Symptoms may fade over a two to twelve-month period when the EMF/EMR is removed or the person moves to a low EMF area.

**Frequency variations:**

Someone suffering EHS may react first to a single frequency source but later to other sources of EMF/EMR due to the increase of transmission, introduction of more Wi-Fi devices or to other electrical equipment that previously had not produced a health effect.

**Intensity of symptoms:**

The level of EHS intensity may increase over time, the longer the person is exposed. A person early on, may be affected by a phone held to the side of the head, but over time be affected by a mobile phone 2-3 metres away.

**Ionising similarities:**

Studies indicate symptoms from exposure to electromagnetic (non-ionising) radiation are similar to those from radioactive (ionising) radiation such as X-rays.

**Severe reactions:**

People experiencing severe reactions could include paralysis, convulsions, seizures, loss of consciousness and stroke. Or exposure may exacerbate an existing medical condition such as Parkinson's disease, MS or affect children on the autism spectrum.

**Variety and differentiation:**

Individual variation in tissue or bone density, acidity, salt content, skin conductivity, and size may affect absorption. This may also relate to the variety of symptoms. Vibroacoustic disease, a medical condition manifested in those who have had continual exposure, (10 years or more), to large pressure amplitude and low frequency noise - less than 500 Hz (infrasound at <20Hz). This disease could lead to heart arrhythmia or death.

Information source: *Electromagnetic Sensitivity and Electromagnetic Hypersensitivity, (also known as Asthenic Sickness, EMF Intolerance Sickness, Idiopathic Environmental Intolerance – EMF, Microwave syndrome, Radio Wave Sickness) A Summary by Michael Bevington. (Capability Books UK.)* [63]

Electrical Sensiticity-UK website is a great website to gain a greater understanding of the health effects. Here you'll find scienctific studies and experts with a history of EHS.

## Reducing dangerous health effects from exposure to EMF and EMR

Preventing exposure where you spend the most time is critical, that's why Building Biology Guidelines aim for safe levels in sleeping areas and workplaces as a priority. Reducing exposure to EMF is extremely important for anyone with an inflammatory illness like chronic inflammatory response syndrome (CIRS) or chronic fatigue sydrome (CFS). Self-responsibility appears the only option since authorities are failing in their duty of care.

Beware of Bluetooth wireless hearing Aides: I have not tested new wireless hearing aides, however during my discussions with other people affected by EMF/RFR I was told about a construction worker in the USA, who suffered a brain injury due to epileptic seizures from wearing Bluetooth hearing aids. Five weeks after he first started wearing the new hearing aids, he suffered a Grand Mal Seizure – one of the worst type. He stopped wearing them for a period of three months up to April 2023, and during this time he had no seizures. When he started a new job in May 2023, he began wearing them again due to work requirements. On September 9 of that year he had another seizure, after wearing them on a regular basis. This was followed by two additional Grand Mal Seizures in December. Consequently he lost his job. His only history of epilepsy was one mild seizure with no lasting effects, as a child. After wearing the Bluetooth hearing aids the epileptic seizures were far worse than anything he had ever experienced in his life, resulting in several trips in ambulances to Hospital Emergency Departments, and time spent in intensive care. It was confirmed, after he underwent a functional brain scan process over two days, at a world class EMF Research Centre in Richardson, Texas, [64] that the Bluetooth hearing aids had contributed to the seizures and it was established that organic brain damage had occurred from these seizures. (Name provided, but withheld for privacy reasons.)

The individual who experienced the seizures, was given no forewarnings of the dangers from this technology. No Safety Data information was issued with the wireless hearing aids, even though scientists around the world have studies indicating EMF may facilitate epileptic seizures [65]

## How many people are affected

In ACADEMIA Letters, an article written by Lauraine Vivian from the University of Edinburgh and Olle Johansson from the Karolinska Institute, express their concern of harm, targeting Elon Musk's…blind vision.[66]

Envisioning a technological singularity, Elon Musk, an industrial engineer, in agreement with the late theoretical physicist Stephen Hawking, argued that in the event of full artificial inteligence (AI) humans could become extinct (Sparkes, 2015). In describing the techno-science driving this paradigm shift, we argue that scientific evidence for harm from electromagnetic radiation (EMR) has been suppressed. This comes as industry has deployed the laws of physics to alter knowledge, changing our relationship to matter.

## The Matter of Harm

This paradigm shift has become inviolable as resource-rich countries hold to its global, democratic benefit and consequently, scientists investigating harm have been silenced. As early as 1988, results from a case-controlled study linking childhood cancer and non-ionizing radiation (NIR) led Savitz et al. to recommend further investigations - they did not get funding. In 2020, Carlberg et al. "postulate that RF radiation is a causative factor for the increasing thyroid cancer incidence" - cancer research funds prioritize funding for a cure and not a causal, genetic trigger ... Similarly, research in the field of electro-hypersensitivity (EHS) remains thwarted. Cindy Sage of Physicians for Safe Technology, has for over two decades witnessed how, "Electrohypersensitive (EHS) people become invisible over time...(they) sought out low-EMF/low-RF environments... always on guard for a new cell tower project or other wireless source... Many are former professionals...give up their careers, lost their homes and became nomads perpetually traveling". One of the current authors, the Swedish Neuroscientist, Professor Olle Johansson estimates that worldwide "around 350 million people" suffer with EHS with the official total reported to be somewhere between 3.5 - 13.3% or...approx. 270 - 1,024 million people.

## Wow! The Mechanisms Of Harm Associated With 5g Is Overwhelming.

In summary, we have sufficient scientific evidence, and actual evidence from canaries, that share their experiences to realise we have an enormous problem that's not going away any time soon. If more than one billion people are affected worldwide, why is this not gaining attention in the media, and the medical industry. This is a worldwide humanitarian emergency. It appears the media and governments will protect Profits @ Any Cost, regardless of the damage caused to innocent people. If business leaders around the world spoke up, we could save an enormous amount of misery and limit further harm.

You are now consciously aware but are you sufficiently competent to tackle prevention or comprehend the enormity of the problems we face. Lets keep learning to master this massive problem of deception, harm and trickery by Profits @ Any Cost.

# CHAPTER 3

# BECOMING SMARTER THAN YOUR SMART PHONE

*"The mind that opens to a new idea never returns to its original size."*

- Albert Einstein

## OVERCOMING 7 THREATS TO A GOOD LIFE - TO GET MORE LIFE OUT OF LIFE

Once upon a time I used to fit in, I followed the modern medical model and did as I was told. That strategy didn't work, it made me sick, then it made me frustrated and then it made me mad enough to pursue the truth and gain a qualification so I could help others wanting answers to problems spiralling out of control. Being smarter turned out to be a lot simpler than suffering. First, you have to understand how the law of cause and effect always works and second, you need to know how Profits @ Any Cost operate.

We'll go back in time to expose historical events and potentially our demise. It's time to look at the results we didn't get. When President Nixon declared war on cancer in 1972, he was talking in code to a secret society; decoding it, he said: let's create a system to hijack truth, poison people and the planet and make billions of dollars along the way. Nixon was not a leader he was part of a secret club, as are others of his kind. That's my opinion and you may disagree, so I'll do my best to help you decide if fitting in is working for you. Unbeknown to me, secret societies including many elites (identified as the Illuminati), are people above government controlling the world. People and organisations, including government agencies under their control, known as the Deep State (DS), commit crimes against humanity all around the world. Once I understood what was going on I realised the humongous problem we had ahead of us, to overcome their dirty deeds. I'll explain more shortly.

## An alternate education opens your eyes to corruption

Studying environmental health exposed cancer-causing agents allowed to be distributed by Profits @ Any Cost companies, without sufficient warnings of the danger to health. This explained why we are not winning the war on cancer, auto-immune disorders or chronic inflammation. An alternative education opened a can of worms (parasites), a can of corruption and a can-do attitude. These three cans need to be investigated.

Wisdom from great leaders must not be ignored, it must be explored.

> "Make a habit of two things: to help; or at
> least do no harm." Hippocrates

Hippocrates (460 BC) often referred to as the father of modern medicine focused on the healing power of nature. He was possibly the first physician to focus on preventing illness suggesting disease is a product of diet, lifestyle and environmental factors. His teachings influenced clinical medicine although, I believe nefarious (evil) influences took over at the beginning of the 20th century.

Charles Darwin suggested; "only the fittest survive." That statement was made before mass toxification of the planet in the 20th century. I believe fitting in is killing us.

"Those who question everything, and learn how to dodge threats to a good life, are the ones likely to survive." ~ Chery Lanne.

## Knowledge is power and a survival strategy

Threats to a good life are everywhere but mostly they are masquerading as good for you. Be prepared to gain a higher level of consciousness. Only when you have higher consciousness can you use it as a shield against threats to life, that once upon a time were invisible.

## # 1: Ideas that seemed like a good idea at the time but are not.

**Modern Medicine:** In 2000 the Journal of the American Medical Association acknowledged the leading cause of death in the USA was iatrogenic illness, which is illness derived from medical treatment. Fact; more deaths are caused annually in the USA, around 783,936, from medical treatment, mis-diagnosis and other causes by a doctor or surgeon including diagnostic procedures, than by heart disease which was responsible for less than 700,000 deaths. It is clear modern medicine could be public health enemy number one. (Source; Dr Bruce Lipton, Spontaneous Evolution). [67]

Statistically 16.4 million people are affected annually by unnecessary medical events in the American medical system. Death by medicine is a fact, not a fallacy according to Null et al. [68] the cost is $282 billion annually. Gary Null PhD, along with four other doctors meticulously reviewed the public literature, and statistical evidence, dealing with deaths caused by government-protected medicine. They identified adverse reactions to prescribed drugs in hospital amounted to 2.2 million per year. Unnecessary prescribed antibiotics per year for viral infections amounted to 20 million. Unnecessary surgery and medical procedures amounted to 7.5 million per year and unnecessary hospitalisations annually amounted to 8.9 million per year. Death by Medicine is real and Profits @ Any Cost are smiling all the way to the bank.

I'll keep this brief because we've already touched on this subject. The Rockefeller and Carnegie Foundations invested millions into medicine and medical education, paid board members of medical establishments and controlled the media. The registration of doctors was used to monopolise treatment of all conditions and diseases. They defined disease as a market place, maintaining a monopoly of the medical industry. The pharmaceutical industry profit from the medical system and from sickness, which is their number one money earner. Don't think for a minute they want you well. This is a sickness system, not a health system.

Chemotherapy agents were first derived from mustard gas used in WWII. Chemotherapy does kill cancer cells, but it also kills non-cancerous cells. In other words, cancer treatment is classed as a carcinogen. An example: Tamoxifen is a hormone therapy drug to treat breast cancer in women and men. It's also called endocrine therapy. Tamoxifen is classified as a carcinogen. This means they treat a health condition with something that is going to give you cancer. No one in their right mind would think this is a good idea.

Dr Samuel Epstein, cancer expert in the USA, and author of *The Politics of Cancer Revisited,* said *"we are not winning the war on cancer, we are losing the war."* [69] The biggest lie they tell is that chemo is the only option, along with radiation. Both are known to cause biological harm. Dr. Rashid Buttar, in an interview with Ty Bollinger in Truth About Cancer Series, pointed out the bleeding obvious; people who administer these drugs need to wear personal protective gear because the treatment is known to be toxic. Why would you give anyone who is already sick, something that is going to make them sick. This treatment doesn't make sense.

This isn't your first lesson in being smarter than your smart phone, but it's a big one. Everyone in Australia (and possibly the world) needs to be aware of how the medical mafia/government agencies work together. If you take your child to the hospital for a diagnosis, you are not permitted to choose an alternative to chemotherapy and radiation if your child is diagnosed with any form of cancer. If you try to use alternative treatment the medical system will alert government agencies who threaten to take your children off you and make them a ward of the state. This is to ensure the child undergoes chemotherapy and radiation treatment. Does that sound like they follow the Hippocratic oath - to do no harm? This fact did not come from a documentary - this fact came from personal experience.

The medical system is rigged against healing naturally. If you kill your immune system, you have no defence against pathogens, which under a normal situation, your immune system knows what it needs to do, because it's designed to heal, and that's what 5G is designed to stop.

You have been tricked. Did you know, when you develop a runny nose, fever, cough, aches and pains, your immune system is already working to fight the pathogen, to save your life. Symptoms are not the cause of disease; they are the warning sign something is wrong. You need to look for the cause and get rid of it. Which leads to number two.

# # 2: CHEMICALS used daily build up in your body over time

Household chemicals cause chronic inflammation and health effects similar to drugs. Inflammation in the body is the beginning of cancer and autoimmune disorders. Inflammation is a warning, not the problem. What causes the inflammation is the problem. Many chemicals known to cause irritation and toxic effects start with P:

- **Parabens:** Widely used preservatives in hair care products, moisturisers, personal lubricants, toothpaste, pharmaceutical and cosmetic products. Also used in food.
- **Polyethylene Glycols and Polysorbate (PEGS):** Polyethylene Glycol is a polymer derived from petroleum. There are hundreds of versions of PEGS, used in skincare, which contain dioxane, known to be toxic. It's been linked with breast cancer, tumours in gallbladder, liver, lungs and more.

- **Perfume:** Includes fragrance, scent and cologne containing dozens of synthetic chemicals known to be hormone disruptors.

- **Petroleum:** Petroleum jelly, mineral oil and other petroleum-based products are virtually the same, they are byproducts of the oil industry. Often sold as a protectant; they block skin pores, meaning your skin doesn't breathe as it should. They are known to contain toxic hydrocarbons absorbed into the body and accumulate in fat cells.

- **Persistent Organic Pollutants:** POP's listed by the Stockholm Convention [70] include pesticides, herbicides, and fungicides. Many are listed by the International Agency for Research on Cancer (IARC) [71] as carcinogenic to humans. IARC is a sister organisation to the World Health Organisation (WHO) set up to investigate cancer causing agents.

- **PFOAS, PFC's, PFASs and Teflon Chemicals:** These chemicals, known as fluorinated compounds, can be found in food, cosmetics, water, firefighting foam and in Teflon which is used in non-stick cooking appliances, pots and pans. Both animal and human studies of fluorinated compounds have links to cancer, kidney disease, liver degeneration, and reproductive system and immune system damage.

- **Phthalates:** Are toxic chemicals in vinyl plastic particularly polyvinyl chloride (PVC).

- **Polychlorinated biphenyls:** PCBs are man-made organic chemicals, toxic to all living things. IARC lists 120 toxins known to cause cancer (Group 1), 82 toxic agents probably carcinogenic to humans (Group 2A), and 302 agents possibly carcinogenic to humans (Group 2B). Reported by WHO 2018, and the list is growing.

- **PVC:** Over the last 40 years, PVC plastic production has grown to over 30 million tons per year (Healthy Building Network Report), [72] causing substantial, never seen before, health hazards and environmental concern. PVC production is the highest user of chlorine gas, of which the feedstock and by-products are highly persistent, (linger in the environment) and are bio-accumulative and toxic. Bioaccumulation means the substance is fat-soluble, building up in the tissue of living things. Toxicity means, the additives and by-products of PVC are known to cause cancer, disruption to the endocrine system, reproduction impairment, birth defects and impaired child development, neurotoxic (damaging to the brain and its function), and immune system suppression. Accidental production of dioxins (the most damaging of all toxins) are released when chlorine-based chemicals are burned or processed under reactive conditions.

Other toxins not starting with P include: **Aluminium**, a neurotoxin found in deodorants, **Triclosan**, found in toothpaste, body wash, hand sanitizers and more. **Triclosan** damages the endocrine system and hormone function, even in very low doses. **Methylisothiazolinone (MIT)** is known to be an allergen, banned in some countries, but can still be found in face moisturizers, sunscreen, foundation and primer, mascara, bronzer and highlighters, body wash, shampoo and conditioners.

Toxins masquerading as good for you can be your worst nightmare. **Talc** used in talcum powder, once used as a deodorant, is now banned, because talc was discovered to be a carcinogen and a leading cause of ovarian cancer, known as a silent killer. Researching court cases against Johnson & Johnson helps to understand how people have learnt the hard way. Johnson & Johnson have paid out millions in compensation but you never hear their stories on the main stream news.

**Fluoride**, added to town water systems, is branded as a chemical to beat tooth decay. What they don't tell you is, it's a neurotoxin, and it can lower IQ in children, sufficient enough for a normal child to be classified as a slow learner. (Fluoride Action Network). [73]

**Formaldehyde**, is found in building products and furnishings, such as particle board, chip board, ply, oriented strand board, medium density fibre board (MDF) used in joinery and many other products like glues, adhesives, carpets, mattresses, bedding and window coverings. Formaldehyde is a known carcinogen. It is used by industry because it has many benefits. It causes irritation to the respiratory system, eyes, skin rashes, nausea and fatigue. IARC classifies formaldehyde as a carcinogen, yet it's allowed to be used in products that go into schools, hospitals, day care centres, and homes without questioning the ethics or integrity of the people making it, supplying it or specifying it in building projects. Look into vaccinations and you will find formaldehyde is an additive. Why?

While we're on the subject of chemicals and I've mentioned vaccines, I'll highlight a presentation by Dr Stephanie Seneff (2018), [74] [75] that totally astonished me. Glyphosate contamination was found in vaccinations, along with aluminium. Alhydrogel (aluminium hydroxide gel) is the main adjuvant (ingredient to create an immune response in vaccinations) licensed for human and animal vaccines. Cumulative vaccinations in childhood appear to be linked to autism spectrum disorder. Dr Andrew Wakefield, from the UK, became a discredited doctor, because he blew the lid on the vaccine industry when he identified a link between enterocolitis (inflammation of the digestive tract) in children and autism following MMR vaccination. Glyphosate and aluminium found in many other vaccinations, including flu vaccines, are linked to impaired gluten metabolism and leaky gut syndrome.

Two very compelling documentaries worth watching, that expose the issues with vaccines are: 1986: The Act (2020) [76] and VAXXED: From Coverup to Catastrophe. Both directed by Dr Andrew Wakefield.[77]

Unfortunately, this list is not conclusive, there's many more toxic agents in everyday products, and they keep making more. One of the biggest problems is they pose a potential danger to our most defenceless life forms, our eggs and sperm, the unborn foetus, our babies and children. What they don't tell you in doctor's surgeries or hospitals is that children and sick people, with a compromised immune system, are greatly affected by chemicals and hospital environments.

**WHERE are they?** Unfortunately, chemicals exist in products most people use on a regular basis, such as laundry detergent, cleaning products, air-fresheners, hand sanitizers, perfume, personal care products, including: deodorants, toothpaste, shampoo, conditioners, moisturisers, sunscreen, make-up, and products used in workplaces, schools, and childcare centres. There's an abundance of nasty chemicals and solvents in paints, glues, PVC building products, and furnishings in new homes. Chemicals off-gas into indoor air mostly when new, however many continue to vaporise over the life of the product. Chemicals produce volatile organic compounds (VOCs) and you've probably smelt them when painting or applying two pack polyurethane or glue used by plumbers and builders.

**WHY they are bad (1)?** Manufactured products contain multiple chemicals, including; pesticides, preservatives, flame retardants, petro-chemicals, and synthetic fragrance. Chemicals end up in the air you breathe in your home and workplace or on your skin, in your clothes, and in your food. If you are unaware of how to stop them, you and your children will end up chemically loaded. Like the proverbial loaded gun ready to go off at any time. Phthalates are known to have irreversible effects on male reproduction because they interfere with male sex hormones and production of testosterone, especially in the early years of life.

**WHY they are bad (2)?** Unsuspecting adults and especially children do not choose their habitat or usually have a say in designing it. Chemicals can produce health effects, cross the blood brain barrier and pass through the placenta just like cigarette smoke, drugs and alcohol. Innocent people purchase toxic products because they are unaware of the danger, or the health effects combinations of chemicals produce, classified as a synergistic effect.

Man designed the legislation allowing these chemicals to inundate our world and it could be their demise because men now have 50% less sperm than they did 70 years ago. Continue heading down the road of infertility and men will need more than Viagra can deliver.

**RESULT:** Chemicals build-up (bio-accumulate, identical to EMF) in the body causing an inflammatory response. Bio-accumulation means cells, tissue, organs, and bones are loaded and you are literally playing Russian roulette if you surround yourself with EMR.

Chemicals affect your gut, your brain, your immune system, and your ability to produce and raise healthy children. Prolonged exposure leads to poor health. Chemicals cause inflammation leading to serious health problems often classified as autoimmune disorders. They start the cancer process although not always on their own. Inflammation is linked to threats #3 and #4. Phthalates mimic the effects of oestrogen in the body, that's why they are classified as hormone disrupting chemicals (HDC). Testicular cancer and breast cancer have links to HDCs. High exposures can lead to reproductive failure, nausea, vomiting, birth defects, endocrine cancers, fertility issues, and more. Phthalates are associated with increased risk of breast cancer, neurological disorders, and attention deficit disorder (ADD), which are examples, and the effects can be transgenerational as chemicals can persist in a mother's body for up to 7 years or longer. No-one links the effects of these chemicals with EMF and how it increases damage to biological cells.

Bioaccumulation triggers inflammation and conditions like chronic fatigue syndrome and irritable bowel syndrome (IBS), multiple chemical sensitivity (MCS) or multiple chemical hypersensitivity. Once good health is lost it is a very slow recovery and has by far the greatest impact on quality of life. MCS disorder is also linked to problem number 3. Refer to the Environmental Working Group [78] for further evidence.

## #3: MOULD growth in water-damaged buildings is a biological toxin

**WHERE is it?** Mould is nature's greatest decomposer both outdoors and indoors wherever moisture exists. Mould is not fussy where it grows or what it feeds on. In water damaged buildings it can be prolific and often undetected by occupants and unseen to the human eye.

Any fibrous material, dirt or dust coming into contact with water or moisture from condensation in cavity walls, ceiling spaces, rising damp, broken or leaking water pipes, flooding, contaminated Heating Ventilation Air Conditioning (HVAC) systems, poor ventilation, leaking roof systems or storm damage is food for mould. High humidity, above 70% relative humidity, can contribute to increases of mould growth on mattresses, curtains, clothes and shoes if the high humidity exists for long periods of time. High humidity and moisture buildup can be caused by poor ventilation in bathrooms and wet areas or because rooms are closed up to reduce heating costs in cold environments. High humidity in tropical climates may also contribute to mould problems in buildings, not designed or maintained to reduce moisture.

**WHY it's bad?** Mould is neither plant nor animal; it belongs to the fungi kingdom. Mould spores exist in the air everywhere but will not grow in buildings or cause damage unless sufficient moisture exists or persists for 48-72 hours or longer. Mould digests whatever it grows on, releasing microscopic spores into the air. Mould growing on wet building materials like plaster, timber and manufactured timber products (chipboard), carpet or furnishings produce microbial volatile organic compounds (MVOCs). MVOCs cause biotoxin-related illness and breathing them in results in inflammation in the body and brain.

24% of the population do not have the ability to create antibodies to fight these toxins. If exposed, susceptible people can be seriously affected. Mould causes long lasting biological damage because of its capability to move from cell to cell through cell membranes. Not many people understand the cost of exposure to their health or their bank balance. Mould can fool you because one person may be fine while another person living or working in the same mouldy building could be constantly sick with numerous health problems that never go away, no matter how much they look after their health or how many medications they take.

Moisture buildup due to condensation, within the building envelope (exterior walls and roof space) in newly constructed energy efficient homes is common. New buildings wrapped in non-breathable fabric (wall wrap), with no ventilation or poor ventilation are highly likely to have fungal growth, exposing occupants to bacteria, mycobacteria, and mycotoxins. These toxins are microscopic, meaning you can't see them, in the air. When mould spores settle on surfaces they can look like dust. 100 mould spores will fit on the head of a pin. It's nearly impossible to eradicate them in soft furnishings, clothing and carpet. Exposure to mould seriously compromises your ability to perform at your best, and for some it's devastating. [79]

Be very careful when opening a bag of potting mix, compost, or mulch products sold in plastic bags. When opened, mould spores infiltrate the air and you'll breathe them in. Using a P2 or P3 face mask is recommended, even for people not susceptible to mould, because they can cause a severe reaction. This immune response is the body's innate intelligence working to eliminate the toxins, and in compromised people, susceptible to mould, the effects can be horrendous.

**RESULT of Mould in a WDB:** Mould affects the central nervous system causing chronic inflammatory response syndrome (CIRS) often misdiagnosed as chronic fatigue syndrome or worse, a mental illness. Not everyone will get CIRS but everyone connected to people who do will be affected in some way.

Exposed adults and children will present with symptoms such as fatigue, body aches and pains, morning stiffness, light sensitivity, blurred vision, sinus problems, cough, shortness of breath, abdominal pain, diarrhoea, memory issues, decreased learning ability, confusion, brain fog, poor concentration, mood swings, anger, numbness, tingling, muscle tremors, skin conditions and vulnerable people may end up with multiple chemical sensitivity and multi-system dysfunction. [80]

## What happens when mould and Wi-Fi mingle?

Kim Goldberg, from British Columbia, Canada, holds a degree in Biology from University of Oregon, and is the creator of Refugium; Wi-Fi Exiles & The Coming Electroplague. Kim posted a video on her website: *Mold Toxins Skyrocket with EMR Exposure.* [81] The video narrated by Dr. Dietrich Klinghardt, revealed what happens to mould when exposed to background wireless radiation. A researcher in Switzerland grew mould cultures in a petri dish under protection of shielding material. He measured the number of mycotoxins they produced on a daily basis. When he removed the shielding material and exposed the mould to the ambient environment, including exposure to a wireless router, computer, lights and a mobile phone tower broadcasting wireless radiation, production of biotoxins in the mould culture increased more than 600 times. Not only did the mould put out more microbial toxins, it produced more toxic biotoxins. This was a huge awakening for Dr. Klinghardt, because it explained why microbes in the body produce more potent biotoxins when exposed to EMR.

Mould spores (fungi) growing in water-damaged buildings feel they are being attacked and their only defence to survive, is to become more aggressive and bitterly hostile to surrounding mould. Mould and wireless radiation are a volatile toxic mix, capable of causing unending misery. Rarely is the cost of water damage understood, whether it's the cost to health, the cost to remediate a water-damaged building, the loss of income or loss of good times. Living in a mouldy building could end up being very costly. (See threat number 4 & 7)

# # 4: SMART TECHNOLOGY (EMR) and the Internet of Things

According to Gay Hendricks, author of The Big Leap, we have a choice to learn in one of two ways.

> **"The universe will teach us our lessons with the tickle of a feather or the whomp of a sledgehammer, depending on how open we are to learning the particular lesson. Getting stubborn and defensive invites the sledgehammer; getting open and curious invites the feather."**

Are we smart enough to dodge the sledge hammer?

## SMART Tech is not smart for us, it's designed to be profitable in multiple ways

Smart technology is marketed as a good thing, along with artificial intelligence (AI) but really it is just a stepping stone to total control through the Internet of Things; SMART cities and SMART technology capturing data and you.

This is an extract from nanowerk.com, about SMART things: [82]

"Originally, the term 'smart' was used as an abbreviation for **S**elf-**M**onitoring **A**nalysis and **R**eporting **T**echnology ... capable of connecting with internet networks and thus connect with other devices or remote databases. But the simple fact that a device that's connected to the Internet or can send and receive information doesn't make it smart yet.

It seems that nowadays everyone has a smartwatch and smartphone, and lives in a smart home that is in a smart city. Every other service and product is 'smart' or 'intelligent' and they have started flooding our lives – undoubtedly the label 'smart' is abused in a not insignificant way."

There is no clear-cut definition of what a smart device is; it definitely is not a technical term. A lot of marketing hype has resulted in misconceptions that anything that contains a computer chip or has some preprogrammed functions is smart.

"For the purpose of our article, we use this definition: **Smart technologies refer to various devices, systems and applications that utilize artificial intelligence, internet connectivity and other advanced technologies to enhance and automate various tasks in various fields such as home automation, transportation, healthcare, security, etc. Examples include smart home devices, smart cities, smart cars, wearable technology and smart healthcare devices."**

The Internet of Things (IoT) is not designed to benefit the people; it is designed to control everyone on the planet.

Nanowerk.com paints an even bigger picture.

"In 1999, British technologist Kevin Ashton came up with the term Internet of Things to define a network that not only connects people, but also the objects around them. At the time, most people thought this was the stuff of science fiction films. Today, the IoT has become a reality, thanks to the development of communication technologies, big data analytics, and ever more sophisticated algorithms."

At some point in 2008 or 2009, the number of things connected to the Internet came to exceed the world's human population. Since then, the IoT has become a vast network of connected objects collecting and analyzing huge amounts of data and autonomously performing tasks. An estimated more than 35 billion devices will be connected by the end of 2021 to this data network worldwide – sensors, household appliances, machines, wind turbines, medical devices, TVs, watches, cars and much more.

According to predictions the number of IoT connected devices will grow dramatically to 75 billion in 2025 and to a staggering 125 billion by 2030. At that point, there will be almost 15 things connected to the Internet for each human on earth."

Thankyou Nanowerk.com

## SMART Devices are Controlling Devices

*Is this Love in the Digital Age*

It seems Profits @ Any Cost have put in place systems that dumbs us down, take away rights, freedoms and the option of choice. Placing chips and wireless transmitters and receivers in products without our permission is scandalous. I've had to disable wireless connections in TV's, air conditioners, smoke alarms, and discontinue use of some products because I couldn't turn off the Wi-Fi. Canaries that took their own lives had no choices left. Could this stupidity increase in the future? Absolutely.

Smart Tech and artificial intelligence (AI) make people senseless and could lead to the downfall of humanity. It is time to rise above the trickery, and take a good hard look at what SMART devices are capable of. Most important question of all is - who controls their capability?

EMR/Wireless technology links us to the world and it seems our modern world cannot live without it. More appliances are linked to smart networks than ever before. Smart home technology, spy cameras, washing machines and dryers, refrigerators, air conditioners, lights, speakers, Google Home, Google Minis, baby monitors, and the list goes on. Soon they'll have them in babies' diapers. Oops, smart diapers already exist.

Additionally, artificial intelligence (AI) can be used for immoral reasons. I was alerted to real world AI capabilities by my internet security program. They provided some facts about AI-generated persons. Apparently, AI-generated persons are used to create fake, yet convincing videos, to infect devices with malware, or to deceive people so their creators can steal money or information. People in these videos only exist online, and it's impossible for normal people to track them down. Fake videos can be created to generate marketing videos, fake trading sites, financial advisers (or a copy of one) offering education and often proposals that seem too good to be true. Always check the video channel, investigate the @handle to see if it matches the real site, because this may indicate a scam. Never do what they suggest, like click on a link or run a command if it looks suspicious.

Deepfakes and AI-generated personas are becoming progressively common, distorting reality, making it difficult to determine who you can trust. Get to know the people you follow and only trust those that have genuine stories and realistic histories. More can be found online, from Gen Threat Labs or other malware sites. [83]

IoT is linked to Internet of Biological Nano Things (IoBNT). [84] The European 5G Public Private Partnership (5PPP) have a vested interest in the physical arena connecting overall architecture, to network management to software networks. Wireless Body Area Networks (WBANs) consists of sensors located on the body, as intelligent patches or implanted in the body, via injections, or smart technology interacting with the body. The ability to control you in ways nature never intended is quite unimaginable by normal people. AI technology, in my opinion, is not designed for you, it's designed for those that want total control.

More context is provided by Sabrina on Odysse, where she exposed U.S. scientists successfully inserting nano-networks into human body cells and have them communicate with microbe-based IoT applications. The goal is to be able to administer drugs via the Internet and monitor and control internal human biological processes in real time. [85]

You can research this topic by searching for Open System Architecture. Open Group SOSA Consortium. Electronic Warfare. Body Area Network (BAN) Wikipedia, and Electronic Signal Transduction. This is scary stuff and I don't want to delve into it because it's not something I can control or provide solutions to fix this overreach, other than to say "stay away from it." Beware, if you go down the rabbit hole of Electronic Warfare, it's a very deep hole and very chilling. We'll concentrate on things we can control.

> *"It's easier to fool people than to convince them they have been fooled"*
> ~ Mark Twain

## #5: MARKETING, PR and PROPAGANDA tricking us all the time

Persuasive marketing, emotional marketing and marketing overloaded with easy, safe, and cheap solutions sold as good for you by people without a conscience, morals, ethics, or knowledge of the danger to human life. Surely there is a law against misleading advertising? Sorry, if the products are allowed to be produced or imported, they are allowed to be sold, no questions asked.

**WHERE does this problem exist?** With products labelled and sold as green, natural, or organic to sway your purchasing decision when they are not. This is not marketing with good intent; this is money-making connected to Profits @ Any Cost.

**WHY it's bad?** Anyone can use green, natural or organic in their marketing without having to prove it's safe. For example; product labels can contain fragrance and perfume in the ingredients list when the fragrance used could contain multiple toxic chemicals not listed, because fragrance secrecy is legal. In reality everything comes from nature, even harmful concoctions and sometimes what you think is safe, is not.

**RESULT:** You could be buying products without knowing the cost to your health, your child's health, or your employees' health. Sadly, what seemed easy or cheap ends up being excruciatingly expensive. Recovery from life-time exposures can cost you years of earnings, mostly because the government doesn't require manufacturers to prove product safety and it's the industries that set the standards, not the people.

If you are unaware of how the PR and propaganda industry works against us, read Toxic Sludge Is Good for You! by John Stauber and Sheldon Rampton. [86] This book blows the lid off the multi-billion-dollar propaganda-for hire industry. It's a tell all book exposing how the politicians and "invisible men" control the media, control debates and public opinion, twisting reality to protect the rich and powerful people and business magnates from scrutiny.

You may not know Governments use the same trick-you tactics by engaging dubious scientists to spread misinformation and paid-for research designed to provide false evidence of no harm. Don't believe anything you read or watch on the nightly news; it's mostly controlled propaganda.

## #6: STRESS: Dis-stress leads to dis-ease

**WHERE it is?** At work, at school, at home; in business, in government, in sporting clubs and in people trying to please everyone all the time.

**WHY it's bad?** Stress overload or constant stress affects you physically and mentally. Good stress is meant to save your life, that's if you're in a tricky situation, and you need a burst of adrenalin to run away from the tiger or fight off the villain stealing your life-savings. The release of cortisol is your body's response to danger. It gives you a burst of energy when you need it most, by increasing your body's metabolism of glucose.

A stress response is not bad for you if your body recovers quickly from the threat or perceived threat. Bad stress is the kind that never goes away when your body produces cortisol via your adrenal glands that sit above your kidneys. Cortisol production is regulated by your pituitary gland located at the base of your brain. It is sometimes referred to as the master gland, because of its vast effects on the body. Symptoms of too much cortisol include weight gain, particularly around your abdomen and irregular menstrual periods, acne, thin and fragile skin that is slow to heal, and it softens ligaments leading to sports injuries. If you don't have enough cortisol, symptoms might be muscle weakness, weight loss, continual tiredness, pain in the abdomen or nausea and vomiting.

**RESULT:** Being in a stressed or anxious state of mind means your body is in a continual state of "fight or flight". Continual stress affects your immune system and makes you sick. It affects your gut microbiome, brain function, and hampers healing and cell regeneration.

# #7: THE COST of getting things wrong

The cost of these Threats to A Good Life are yet to be determined. What will be the cost to children or their ability to have children? Or how many more people will receive a mis-diagnosis and end up on the *death by medicine* data base?

### *"Power corrupts and absolute power corrupts absolutely" quote by Lord Acton.*

Regulators and politicians have a vested interest in keeping quiet or letting industry decide. If people lose their ability to earn a decent income or are unable to work as they once could, the government will need an enormous budget to fund the crooked pharmaceutical/medical system, social services, pensions, schools, aged care and Medicare. They know this yet they allow industry to set their own standards and dictate standards based on their own agenda. As one official report suggested "we do not want to induce panic," but they are ok with death by medicine, and loss of life and livelihood from chemicals and EMF.

**WHERE is the problem?** The problems are in the systems of governance we are required to follow in blind faith. Industries set their own standards, with a vested interest in Profits @ Any Cost, and nothing else. This is a construct of the industrial revolution. and those in the know, like G. Edward Griffin, author of The Creature from Jekyll Island, [87] have been warning people for decades.

**WHY it's bad?** Most people do not have the cash, the energy or the time to fight the systems that control us. Profits @ Any Cost win by default because we think we have no power over big corporations, governments or the systems they set up to control our thinking, our spending and our lack of human rights.

**RESULT:** Lives are lost early, and people lose quality of life, as well as the ability to make different choices, however the greatest cost could be the loss of our children's future potential. Many have lost their ability to earn a living while corporate giants grow financially fatter and less accountable.

Survival of the smartest has superseded fitting in. Learning how to dodge this nasty list of threats to life and livelihood is the key to gaining control of the natural order of life. We need to be smarter and we need a plan.

**Confucius may have got it right when he said, "We have two lives, and the second begins when we realise, we only have one."**

## CONTROLLING THE INVISIBLE BEAST

Everyone can make a choice and decide what they're willing to be exposed to. Chemicals, I believe, are way easier to dodge than EMF/RFR. For that reason, it's even more important to increase your level of learning, and that's what this book is designed to deliver. If you're feeling unwell or not sure if wireless radiation is having an effect on you, take a holiday in a remote location with no Wi-Fi, or go camping for a week or more, away from telephone towers and unplug from technology. Keep your phone turned off and only use it for emergencies. Use the holiday as a test to see if you feel better. It may take a week or two or more for your body to recuperate, sufficient enough for you to notice.

EMR can have a lasting effect and in some cases may take three to seven days to feel different. Some feel it immediately when Wi-Fi or phones are turned off. I'm one of those people that detect the frequencies, as if someone is hitting me in the throat, or head with an ice pick, and when devices are turned off the pain goes away. EHS symptoms may start out as a tickle in your throat, causing a cough, cold and flu symptoms, or it may feel like you've hit old age with a vengeance, only you are not old. Everyone is different. For some the pain may be instant, for others it may be insomnia or unexplained fatigue. Or you could have anger management issues, forgetfulness or lapses in memory.

Beware of wireless technology built into caravans. Many are fitted with smart monitors connecting transmitters to numerous devices connected to a smart panel. All wireless connections need to be deactivated, turned off or unplugged to reduce exposure, enabling recovery. Solar inverters in caravans can be hidden under the bed and hard to get at. If you're buying one, make sure it's placed well away from the bed and it's easy to reach, so you can turn it off when sleeping. You definitely don't want to be sleeping above wireless devices or a switch mode power supply; when an inverter is running it will produce DE and EMF and if connected to Wi-Fi, you'll be swimming in RFR.

Protecting the home environment is critical. After being exposed at work, mixing with the public in shopping centres, medical centres, and hospitals, in schools, sporting arenas and city areas, recovery is critical, especially overnight. If your home is a safe environment your body can detox and rejuvenate from RFR and ELF exposure during the day.

Short of chucking your mobile phone in the bin and moving off-grid into the wilderness, like some people have done, the only choice is to implement life-saving strategies. Making your home safe is a major cancer and disease prevention strategy. The following steps allow you to achieve reduction from exposure. It may be beneficial to use shielding between you and the sources of RFR, but only with professional testing and advice to understand what you hope to achieve, or cannot achieve, depending on the location or complexity of the situation. George and I compiled this list and we know it works. Prevention is up there with oxygen, critical for survival.

## IN THE LIVING SPACE:

1. **Make sure your wireless modem/router is connected with a wired connection to your internet and wired to your computer with Wi-Fi turned OFF.** When turned on, wireless radiation exposes everyone, including animals, and your next-door neighbours to harmful RFR. Wireless radiation includes Wi Fi, Bluetooth and Hotspot frequencies from devices. Exposure

at night disrupts your biological systems. Over time - it could be twelve months to ten years, the RFR affects your nervous system (axonal nerves and myelin sheaths) causing it to breakdown, leading to the deterioration of cellular membranes and serious life-threatening disorders. Many new modems are dual band, meaning they use 4G and 5G signals. Often there is a button to turn off Wi-Fi which only turns off one signal, not the other, I discovered this on a Telstra supplied modem. The dual system is designed to be used for anyone in the vicinity to connect with Telstra smart connect, which means you're supplying a wireless connection to anyone on a Telstra connect plan. It could also be used to spy on you. I learned this the hard way and switched to an old Netgear modem which had to be reconfigured. Often the second wireless signal is a 5G frequency and is not detectable without a 5G radiofrequency analyser. Honestly, Profits @ Any Cost have no intention of looking out for you, physically, mentally or biologically.

2. **At work or for a home office, connect your modem to your computer with an Ethernet cable and disable all Wi-Fi.** Put your laptop or computer in flight mode. Turn off Wi Fi and Bluetooth, on your computer in settings. If you have other devices, such as printers, smart TV or multiple computers, invest in a switch box which is a device with multiple Ethernet ports, used to wire all devices directly to the modem. If you have a dual band modem, and you can't test to see if the 2nd wireless signal is off, place the modem in a metal box designed for electrical cabling or place in a mesh cage. I discovered dual band modems don't turn off the 2nd frequency, during testing. You can purchase metal cages from electricsense.com, or a metal box from a hardware store. Engage an electrician or communications expert to install if you're unsure how to do it. Metal boxes should always be mounted on a timber board, not on a metal frame or a metal wall. You may be able to ask your internet provider to turn off the extra 5G transmitter on your modem, but you need

to test to be sure it's safe. These steps will reduce exposure, and provide a healing sleep sanctuary, and a safe work environment. **Note:** If you have a DECT phone (cordless phone), ditch it and replace it with a normal corded non-wireless phone and connect the phone cable to a phone line if you have one, or purchase a voice over internet (VoIP) modem and connection plan with an internet provider, which means you are talking over the internet. It's cheaper to make calls on VoIP than a landline account. Use an old hard-wired phone, not a cordless phone. I use a Uniden phone with handset, but usually use the speaker mode because I don't like anything with wires near my head.

3.  If wireless internet is needed at times, to download a movie, games or to do phone updates, turn on Wi-Fi when needed. At all other times keep your modem's Wi-Fi turned off and keep your computer in flight mode. Ensure Apps (software), including Bluetooth and other emitting programmes are off when not in use.

4.  **Switch to a USB connected keyboard**, mouse and wired printer, and turn off Wi-Fi on printers. If your printer doesn't allow you to turn off Wi-Fi, turn the printer off at the power point and only turn it on when you need to use it. I turn my printer off when not in use, and unplug it. **Note:** If you are unable to do this, you could buy older, safer equipment and devices on EBay, such as: USB printers, wired keyboard, and a ball mouse. Sometimes old technology can be much safer than new technology, but not always. LED screens are safer than plasma screens and old CRT (Cathode Ray Tube) monitors. Remember distance from devices is your friend.

5.  Begin to use new safety rules in your home. Use three pin plugs, especially on computer leads, because **the earth pin helps reduce EMF**. Get into the habit, if you're not using electrical items unplug them from the power point. Keep the majority of your electric appliances, gadgets and non-essentials turned OFF, and disconnect the power plug from the wall, which helps

to reduce RFR and ELF exposure within your home especially if you spend time in close proximity to electrical equipment. Many appliances are smart and emit RFR, without anyone realising it. **Turn off Wi-Fi and Bluetooth settings on your smart TV in settings**, and connect to the internet with an Ethernet cable. Pass-through powerline adaptors may help if the internet is not in the same room as the modem. Consult an expert if you need help. If using iPads or tablets connect the devise using a USB Ethernet connection or download the game or movie and play or watch in flight mode. New devices may have a 5G signal/receiver that doesn't turn off when in flight mode so go into settings to turn off the 5G connection or contact the maker of the product for help or search the internet for solutions. **Note:** Outside sources of electrical harm will come into your home, as DE/EMI (electromagnetic interference) and RFI (radiofrequency interference), via the outside power lines, from other wireless devices and cell towers, sub-stations and transformers. If you are concerned about DE/EMI, call an expert to have your house tested with specialised equipment. There are solutions, such as inline filters on your main electricity line, but it needs to be tested before and after to know it works and that you are safe. Inline filters do not eliminate 100% of DE, but a reduction is always beneficial. Call an expert. Information is available on wellintent.net.

6. **Always place your laptop/notebook on a table or small desk** when using it, not on your lap. A laptop connected to a power supply zaps you with EMF and RFR if wirelessly connected. I also suggest using a wired mouse not the touch pad. In the past using a touch pad on a laptop caused uncomfortable tingling in my fingers and a wireless mouse caused swelling in my fingers and joints. I have recovered, and my fingers have returned to normal. Prevention is a wise move, rather than trying to reverse the damage.

7.  Natural barriers outside are hedges, trees, bushes and plant growth around your home. Trees will absorb and slightly minimise the outside sources of RFR. **Note:** The theory of indoor houseplants protecting you and your family from RFR exposure is a myth, or maybe planted misinformation.

## BEDROOM

8.  **Electric blankets and electric beds emit high levels of EMF,** even if they are turned OFF, they will still emit ELF. The interwoven copper heating elements, metal coils and wiring of an electric blanket act as a conductor for RFR exposure, which is another reason not to use an electric blanket. Built in lights on your bedhead or bedside expose you to high levels of ELF. Switch to USB rechargeable orange bedside lamps available from blockbluelight.com.au in Australia and blockbluelight.com in the USA.

9.  All metal bed frames are a conductor which means the metal will attract EMF in close proximity to an electrical source and reflect EMR. **Consider switching to a wooden bed and a non-spring coil mattress.** Metal spring mattresses act as a conductor for RFR and ELF.

10. Use a battery-operated alarm clock, and **stop using your phone as an alarm clock, unless it is placed in a remote location on flight mode, or in a faraday bag.** Please be aware some new 5G enabled phones will not turn off the 5G signal on flight mode. You may be able to turn it off manually in settings. Contact the maker of the phone if you need guidance, and have it tested to be sure, or keep it in a faraday bag overnight. This way you can still use the alarm function. Faraday bags are made of metal mesh coated with material. Or use a metal tin or a stainless-steel pot. Metal blocks RF but can increase EMF. It's tricky, so seek expert advice if needed.

11. Turning OFF wireless devices at night, may not always work. There are Apps that will turn your phone back ON. If that is so, you will know if your phone has automatically turned back on when you wake in the morning. You may notice the battery charge has declined if it's not on a charger. This means it's been working through the night trying to detect signals from Apps left on. Never use a mobile phone while it's plugged into a charger. It will deliver a high dose of EMF as well as RFR.

## EVERY DAY LIVING

12. Cut down your mobile phone use as much as possible, mainly because RFR exposure from a mobile phone held to your head can cause serious life-threatening disorders, such as cancer and brain tumours over time. Avoid long conversations on your phone. I have a phone cover on my phone that contains metal mesh and only use it for texting or accepting two step verification when absolutely needed. I cover my phone using Naturell shielding fabric purchased from Safe Living Technologies Canada, [88] or Safer EMF, EMR Australia or Gigahertz Solutions in Germany. [89] [90] When using a phone cover for your phone, keep the cover closed and use on speaker setting when talking on the phone. Point the phone away from people if you can and not towards a metal building because RFR reflects off metal.

13. Mobile phone radiation reduction covers are available from multiple places worldwide. [91] Please be aware, I don't recommend using mobile phones as your main connection to the internet, especially if you have signs of EHS, or suffer from existing health disorders. Never let children play with mobile phones unless you are sure you have turned off all wireless connections. Educate them to be smarter than the smart phone.

14. If you use earphones, used wired ones, **don't use wireless Bluetooth earbuds or headphones**, that's like putting a

wireless radiation device next to your brain. Not a good idea. As suggested above, it's best to keep wireless devices away from your brain, that includes other ear pieces, such as wireless hearing aids.

15. When in standby mode, **keep your phone away from your body. Note:** don't place your phone in your breast pocket or bra, or next to your reproductive organs. Testicular cancer is on the rise and lowered male fertility is increasing. When the signal on your phone is one or two bars, it means you have a weak signal, and your phone will emit higher levels of RFR to search for a signal, and emit more RF during a call. Turn your phone off when it's on your body or leave it at home or in your vehicle turned off. Mobile phones are used as a tracking device, not for your benefit. It's best to put your phone on flight mode and return calls when you need to, in a safe location. If you use a shielded pouch, it will still be trying to connect and receive transmissions, therefore they are not 100% safe.

16. For people with signs of electrical hypersensitivity or symptoms of an autoimmune disorder it would be beneficial to reduce all forms of RFR in your environment. Do away with your mobile phone as a main connection to the internet. **Use a computer connected to a modem with an Ethernet cable**. Invest in professional help to detect where the RFR is coming from outside the home and detect where EMF is dangerous inside the home. You may be able to paint walls and ceilings with shielding paint, hang shielded fabric over windows or cover the window panes with RF film, but you cannot introduce any wireless technology into the home. Shielding a whole house creates a faraday cage. That means all visitors to the home must turn off their mobile phones, iPads and tablets because the home will work like a microwave oven, causing signals to bounce around. Metal cladding on walls has the same effect. Living in high-rise buildings with multiple sources of exposures could be the worst-

case scenario for people in the early stages of EHS, or diagnosed with cancer or an autoimmune disorder.

17. **Microwave ovens** were once called radiation ranges (ovens), but no one wanted one. Radio waves heating food was an accidental discovery. During World War II, a self-taught scientist, Percy Spener contributed to developing efficient radar systems (or that's the story they tell). Radar systems used magnetrons to produce frequencies in the microwave range. At the end of the war they (supposedly) needed to find an alternative use for magnetrons. During his experiments Spencer accidently melted a chocolate bar in his pocket because he was standing next to an active radar. He was amazed at the heating effect and tested the microwaves by popping corn and heating an egg that exploded leading him to create a metal box to contain the radiation. This led to changing the name of the oven to a microwave oven. Named after the electrical energy waves used to heat food. Actually, microwaves don't cook food by heating the food with a radiant heat source like a flame or electrical element, they shoot microwaves into the food. Microwaves are extremely adept at exciting and vibrating water molecules, and since food is mostly water, the microwaves create intermolecular friction which generates heat, sufficient enough to cook food. The first microwave ovens caused hot and cold spots created by interference of microwaves. Blackened food was a result until they introduced turntables, enabling the food to be cooked uniformly.

**Food cooked by microwaves causes all life-energy in the food to be lifeless**, with no nutritional value (life-force-energy in food is critical for life). A nurse in a hospital was heating breast milk in a microwave oven to give to prem babies. The babies didn't thrive; they went backwards. Instead, the nurse put the milk in a glass container in a pot of hot water to warm up, and when fed to the babies they began to improve. This is not common knowledge. Ditch your microwave and use old fashioned methods to cook or defrost your food; your body will thank you. Hint: our bodies are 70-75% water which makes them suitable to be cooked by microwaves in the environment. We're not cooked yet, but our bodies definitely absorb the frequencies and I guarantee microwave energy produces an unwanted effect.

18. About enclosures: if you use a mobile/cell phone in a plane, train, tram. motor vehicle, or **any metal enclosure, you will be exposed to the microwave oven effect.** That means when your phone is turned on, even if you're not making a call, the phone is continuously transmitting and receiving signals. Every phone has multiple connections, for data roaming, GPS, location services, text and phone calls, continually searching for a signal or sending location information. This means the signals will be continually bouncing around in the vehicle or train or plane trying to connect. RF bounces off metal; it's called reflection, in the same way microwaves bounce off the metal walls inside a microwave oven. Microwaves are absorbed into anything liquid. You and your kids and babies are 70% water and will be exposed to more RF inside a metal enclosure than outdoors, so my tip is to keep your phone turned off in vehicles at all times, and do not connect to Bluetooth, or let other people, especially kids or teenagers Hotspot other devices inside a vehicle.

When Bluetooth in vehicles was introduced, it seemed like a good idea because it allowed people to answer their phones while driving, however I discovered it multiplies microwave RF exposure. Ever wondered why so many people have road rage these days? Apart from being stressed and frustrated with life, wireless technology has a direct effect on your brain, making it harder to think clearly or deal with emotional issues. Years ago, I had anger issues after driving for a couple of hours in the greater Melbourne area and didn't realise it was related to RFR. The same thing happened to another Building Biologist after an EMF assessment. On a group zoom chat, I asked if any other

Building Biologists had experienced issues of EHS and Steve, one of the nicest guys you will ever meet, said he'd had a road rage incident, after conducting an EMR assessment near a phone tower; something totally out of character for such a nice guy. Be smart, be safe and switch off wireless technology in your vehicle and put your phone on flight mode even if it's in a radiation safe pouch while driving.

*"I have no doubt in my mind that, at the present time, the greatest polluting element in the earth's environment is the proliferation of electromagnetic fields."* Dr Robert O. Becker, Nobel Prize nominee

## Negatives of Blue Light at Night

**Blue light** emitted from computer screens, iPads, tablets, and smart phones produces a negative biological effect. Apart from negative effects of radiation from screens when you sit too close to them, non-native blue light from screens at night reduces production of melatonin, and disrupts sleep. [92] An option is to watch less screens after sunset, or use blue blocking glasses. [93] Another option is to turn on amber light on your screen(s) as the sun sets and turn off again at sunrise. Download software to change screen colour at: 9 Free Blue Light Filters for Desktop Windows PC, Apple Mac and Chrome Browser. [94] (Cannot guarantee safety of this site). You can use amber lights at night to mimic the suns natural orange glow in the evenings, preparing you for sleep.

According to neurosurgeon Dr. Jack Kruse, natural light is healthy light. Getting a dose of sunlight morning noon and night is biologically beneficial. Sunlight is a natural calcium-channel blocker that alters the firing rate of voltage-gated channels on cells. In short, indoor living leads to depression and suicide, while getting outside in the sun and clean air reduces anxiety and depression and improves oxygenation.

## NATURAL HEALTH SOLUTIONS FREE FROM NEGATIVE SIDE EFFECTS

Years ago, I was just like everyone else and didn't believe I would be affected by EMF. That all changed when I had a near death experience in January 2021, after holidaying in an off-grid house (using solar energy) in the Blue Mountains in New South Wales. The electricity meter and inverter were inside a locked meter box and I couldn't turn off the power at night. I woke on our last day with a horrible bloodshot eye and suspected dirty electricity was the cause.

On the road trip from the Blue Mountains to Kangaroo Valley in New South Wales, I began to experience excruciating pain, which started in my legs and progressively moved up my body, until my whole body started to shake uncontrollably. Moving my legs was near impossible and the pain was unbearable. My senses were telling me to get out of the car, so we pulled over at a park outside Goulburn and I laid down on a towel on wet grass to see if I'd recover. For ages I couldn't move, the pain was still intense, and it didn't ease, until I asked for my shielding fabric to be thrown over me. Almost instantly I stopped shaking, which meant there must have been a telephone transmitter nearby.

After about an hour on the ground I attempted to get up. It felt like I'd been run over by a Mack truck, exhausted, aching and moving like a praying mantis, I tried to walk around to recover and regain function, but it had taken a great toll on my body, which explains what bio-accumulation is and how it affects you. Thankfully I survived, but it scared the life out of me. This was the sledge hammer effect. I had a case of over exposure and stupidity; we had our phones on in the car, in shielding cases but we hadn't turned them off. This was one of the biggest lessons of my life. I now consider exposure to wireless radiation, DE and EMF as a threat to life. Even small exposures have caused big issues. I've had two heart attacks and persistent chronic fatigue from shopping in a city area and having my eyes tested at an optometrist that had no idea wireless tech was dangerous. His office was full of it. So, if anyone thinks 4G and 5G transmissions are safe, they're kidding themselves. Bioaccumulation is real and any canary will testify to that.

Over the years I've read oodles of books, research papers and taken countless courses to find solutions. My focus has been on health, longevity, and more recently; how to beat the EHS nightmare!

## Here are my TOP TIPS to be healthier and smarter than your smart phone:

**Earth daily:** This means take your shoes off and put your bare feet directly onto the ground. Green grass is best and adding water, or walking in the water at the beach is even better. Use your commonsense and don't Earth with your phone in your hand or turned on nearby. Earthing allows your body to release negative energy trapped in your cells/tissue. The Earth's magnetic field has a beneficial effect on inflammation. You need to do this in a non-toxic environment. At the beach or in natural bushland or parkland is best where there are no telephone towers in sight, or overhead high voltage power lines or underground cables.

One day on a tram stop in Melbourne, near Flinders Street train station I felt unwell and took readings with my gaussmeter. The EMF was extreme, 48 mG. That's huge, 0.2 mG is healthy. There is no way you would gain a benefit from Earthing in a city environment when you're constantly surrounded by EMF and RFR. You can learn more about Earthing by reading Clint Ober's book, *Earthing; the most important health discovery ever.* [95] [96] I Earth every day and if I can't sleep at night, I will head outside with a couple of blankets and sit under the stars for twenty minutes or more with my feet on the grass. When I return to bed, I fall asleep almost immediately and often do no not wake until morning. It's the best sleeping pill ever.

**Learn the art of controlling your mind through meditation:** When I first started meditating, I had a huge problem trying to turn off my thinking, because I'd read a book suggesting that was required. You can't turn off your mind, that's impossible. I've mastered the art of meditation by controlling my breath and focusing my thoughts. Sit in a comfortable chair away from other distractions. I like to sit on a camp chair on the grass, surrounded by nature with my bare feet on the ground, that way I get a double whammy. Calm your body by taking three deep breaths. Count to four breathing in and count to six breathing out. You need to breath out for longer than you breath in. Slow deep breaths carry more oxygen into the body and a long breath out releases negative energy. You can even tell your body to release negative energy as you do it. Your body listens to what you say/think. Oxygen is one of your weapons against disease. When you first do this, don't think of anything else, just your breath. The aim is to engage your parasympathetic nervous system; this is your rest and repair state. You will know you are in this state because you will need to swallow, usually after three deep breaths. Focus your mind on slow breathing, count 4-5 in and 6-8 out. Out breathes must be longer. Once you're in this calm state think of all the things you are grateful for. Do not think of anything that upsets you. Focus on something you love. It could be your children, grandchildren, a place you like to be, or something you love to do or something you're grateful for. Love has a frequency and it's calming to the body. Anger, disgust and fear all have frequencies that are bad for the body, that's why you must not allow anything upsetting to influence you while you meditate. Continue for at least three minutes, longer if you wish, however three minutes is sufficient time to engage the parasympathetic nervous system, which triggers release of beneficial neurotransmitters from the heart to flood the body, and it has a lasting effect. Your heart does more than pump blood. It has a brain and a memory and an energy field. Love yourself unconditionally, no matter what others have told you. Be kind to yourself and be kind to others, it makes a huge difference if you release negative thoughts. Holding a grudge can have negative effects, energetically, mentally and biologically.

**EFT - Emotional Freedom Technique**: EFT called Tapping is a method to release negative energy, trapped in your body. Negative life experiences produce energy that may get trapped in the body, often in areas where pain is experienced, such as the heart, abdomen, hips etc. Negative energy caused by trauma, stress, anger, or people that put you down, can have a lasting effect. Dawson Church wrote Mind to Matter,[97] a book illuminating the astonishing science of how your brain creates material reality. It is fascinating research and well worth reading. Dawson teaches EFT/ Tapping and I've found it to be hugely beneficial. [98] If you struggle to do it yourself, seek the services of a trained practitioner. I had an experience with an EFT practitioner prior to studying Building Biology and he helped me overcome my fear of failing. It worked, I qualified and it removed many doubts I had about being successful. Anyone can be successful, it just takes persistence, good teachers, mentors or coaches and never giving up.

**Exercise:** I discovered how beneficial exercise was for health in my thirties. Once you get over the initial hard work to build strength and heart lung capacity, exercise is like taking a happy pill. My recommendation is to find something you love to do. If going to the gym is not your thing, that's ok. Move to music you love, preferably not heavy metal because the frequency is not beneficial or healing. Doing what you love means you're more likely to continue to do it, because consistency is key. It could be bushwalking, swimming, bike riding, tennis, Qi gong, dance or a martial art. Even gardening can be beneficial if exercise is not your thing. Yoga is more meditation (mind and breath control) and stretching than aerobic exercise (requiring oxygen) that gets your heart pumping, but if that's what you like, that's ok. You need a bit of huff and puff to gain heart strength and increase lung capacity. Moving your body shifts the blood from internal organs to your extremities. Any aerobic exercise increases your heart rate, feeds oxygen rich blood to your outer extremities and capillaries and reduces stress levels. Long distance running releases endorphins; feel good hormones, often called a runners' high.

Aim to exercise 3-5 times per week. Do it with friends if you don't like exercising alone. If you're older, or have never exercised before, take it slow in the beginning. To be safe, you should always be able to hold a conversation. Exercising with a friend, on your same wave length or fitness level may help. Turn it into a regular activity is my suggestion. When exercising, don't stretch or lift heavy objects before you have warmed up, because cold bodies lack blood flow and injuries are more likely. Blood flow to your muscles warms them up and gives them flexibility. If you become breathless, you're going too hard. You should always be able to hold a conversation. Keep to relatively flat terrain. Build strength slowly before venturing into the hills or undertaking long treks. Simply, move it or lose it, with your phone turned off. Some phones will emit RF when in flight mode. Make exercise your 'me' time but ensure it's free of EMR. Moving to music can be fun, but not if it's through a streaming App disrupting every cell in your body. You can listen to music saved on your phone while it's on flight mode. No wireless connection needed. And definitely don't listen or use wireless Bluetooth ear buds or headphones.

**Build brain power:** Learn something new, it could be a new skill, puzzles or games, or whatever takes your fancy as long as it makes you think. You may want to study to increase your earning potential, or invest in online education to sharpen your brain power.  The old saying "use it or lose it" is just as true for your brain, as it is for your body; it needs to be exercised to keep it functioning well. Your brain never stops changing. It's called neuroplasticity. The only time you're too old to learn something new, or change your brain, is when you're dead. I recommend reading *You Are the Placebo*, [99] and *Becoming Supernatural* by Dr. Joe Dispenza.[100] EFT and Joe's meditation techniques won't stop the effects of wireless radiation, but they help you deal with trauma and initiate inner healing.

**Eat a rainbow:** Include organic vegetables and fruit, nuts and seeds in your diet; choose grass-fed meat (organic if possible), and sea-run fish, not farmed fish if you can help it. Aim to consume 30 different colours per month. I had the pleasure of meeting Chris Woollams, the founder of Cancer Active in the UK in 2014. Chris is the author of, ***Everything you need to know to help you beat cancer*** [101] and ***The Rainbow Diet.*** *[102]* Chris was a very successful business man until his daughter, Catherine, was diagnosed with a brain tumour at 19 and given six months to live. He handed his business to others and researched what he needed to know to keep her alive. Doctors treating Catherine, asked what he'd done, because no one had survived this type of brain tumour for that length of time, which was four years. The result was CancerActive.org, a website designed to help people overcome cancer, which became his passion. Sadly, Catherine died in her mid-twenties, but his quest to help others has not waned.

**Read labels:** This means anything you buy in a packet or a box. You will find most processed food contains artificial ingredients. I mentioned MSG (621) previously; however, many preservatives, artificial colours, sweeteners and flavours are toxic to the body. Preservatives, added to products to increase shelf life, can interfere with your good gut bacteria, needed for optimal gut health. I recommend researching this subject. Read the Chemical Maze Shopping Companion by Bill Statham [103] or browse the Environmental Working Group (EWG) website. [104] Search for safer personal care products, made with love by people who care about health and wellbeing.

**Create a healthy home environment:** Breathing in fumes and particulates from wet applied products containing chemicals, pesticides, fungicides, including perfumes and washing detergents will not lengthen your life. Get rid of Roundup/Glyphosate, chemically loaded laundry detergent, air fresheners and toxic cleaning products in your cupboards and replace with non-toxic products purchased from a health food store or make your own by using vinegar and water and bicarbonate of soda. Use natural organic essential oils with no added chemicals. Eucalyptus oil cleans off sticky labels and disinfects as does tree tea oil. Research healthy non-toxic options. Use alternative methods to deal with garden pests if you like to garden or grow vegies. The list of chemicals in household products is so great I cannot list them here. You can find research on BPA, dioxins, atrazine, fire retardants, arsenic, lead, organophosphates and glycol ethers online, but really, it's just easier to buy certified naturally organic products and organic personal care products from a reputable health food store or online organic products store. Replace nasty skin care products that contain hormone disrupting chemicals with certified organic, natural, non-toxic products. Use zinc-based sunscreen instead of chemically loaded pharmaceutical based products. Learning to read labels could save you a lot of miserable years. I suggest listening to Dr Stephanie Seneff expose the truth about Glyphosate on YouTube, [105] [106] to understand how it impacts gut health and the immune system.

**Mind the company you keep:** During my search for truth about cancer and disease, I discovered some secrets to longevity. I'll tell you more in Chapter 4, but one of the things known to make people sick is the continual lack of self-worth and loneliness. People putting you down or never letting you have your say has detrimental effects. Loneliness can creep up on you as you age, when family move away or your friends are few and far between. I recommend joining groups, become a volunteer in your community or join a club that gets you out and about. Since I've become electrically hypersensitive my options are very limited. To solve that problem, I've joined groups online that provide information about things that matter to me. Wellintent.net might be a good place to hang out, if you're interested in sharing and caring, and love learning cool things.

**Talk to the Universe, it listens:** Quite a few years ago I completed a course on Geobiology also known as geomancy. This training covered divination of the Earth's energy fields to detect geopathic stress and identify harmful or beneficial Earth energy. I learnt how to dowse for answers with a pendulum and make remedies to clear geopathic stress or shift negative energy left behind in rooms in a home or on a property. Dowsing fascinated me, even more so when I discovered (after doing more training) you can ask the universe for answers to questions you don't know. It does take some practice and it's necessary to ask questions that provide a yes or no answer. I use it to ask all sorts of questions and I'm amazed at the answers I get. I gained insight into other aspects of dowsing from Raymon Grace, [107] founder of the Raymon Grace Foundation and speaker at various dowsing conferences.

**The Universe is made up of energy, frequency and vibration and energy holds information (like the data transmitted by technology).** I realised the Universe knows (also known as the quantum field or the aether) and it responds when you ask a specific question. Often when you request information it will be delivered straight to your pendulum or your brain and sometimes it will come to you in other forms. You may not know it, but the Universe listens (others might call it God, the prime creator, higher self, spirit guides, angels, or Source energy), and if you ask for what you want it may well deliver it. Being aware of how it works is part of why it works. Information can land in your lap when you least expect it but you must use discernment (ability to make a smart judgement). Don't ask for things that are unethical, it won't work, like Lotto numbers. And mind your words, don't ask for what you don't want. It can't be relied on to be 100% accurate but it can be a guide or provide a useful assessment if used appropriately.

**Water magic:** Life gives you clues, to master life, if you pay attention. In 1992, I was given the option to have my fourth baby in a bath, at the NW Private Hospital in Burnie, Tasmania. Ruth Forrest, my midwife suggested water would ease my labour pains. At the time I was not aware of waters pain relief potential. I had two babies in hospitals in two different cities and my third baby was born at home, because I was told, at a different hospital in a different city, that the baby wasn't coming yet and to go home and come back later. I tried to resist because my other births had been very quick, but they kicked me out of the birthing unit anyway. When I got home my waters broke and minutes later, our third son was born outside in the freezing cold, as I was getting in the car. The sister in charge at the hospital had told my husband to bring me back to the hospital, and he believed he was doing the right thing.

Baby number four was a different scenario in a different hospital. Ruth seemed to know her stuff so I decided on a water birth. Best decision ever, because the baby was posterior, which means he was around the wrong way (sideways). Normally doctors would use forceps to turn the baby, however I was fit and healthy and Ruth told me my body would know what to do, as long as I could handle a longer labour. During labour I had to get out of the bath to go to the toilet and when I did the pain was quite intense, so I quickly hopped back in and like magic, the pain subsided. I stayed in the bath until he was born and didn't require pain relief or stitches, as I had with previous births. My experience with the magic of water, made me wonder why all expectant mothers are not advised about the benefits of giving birth in a bath. This needs to be questioned.

Building Biology training covers water pollution and water treatment chemicals and filtration, but not the magic of water. Water holds magnetic charge, detectable by watching water droplets bead together down a windscreen. What's even more interesting is the fourth phase of water, beyond solid (ice), liquid and vapour (steam/fog), discovered by Gerald Pollack and Gilbert Ling. [108]

Gilbert Ling taught Gerald Pollack, that water in the cell is nothing like water in a glass. Gerald wrote a book, The Fourth Phase of Water, and in it he explains everyday mysteries about water. Why does your ankle swell up when you break a bone in it? Why can a tree root, that's mainly water, break a concrete path? Why does wet sand hold together, when you build sand castles, and dry sand doesn't? These are just some of the everyday mysteries he explains.

Gerald's book illuminates many things but the most interesting thing I learned is how water contains ability to hold memory, charge (as in energy), and it creates an exclusion zone, known as EZ water, which helps explain the function of our cells, to provide energy when we need it. Humans are approximately 70% or 2/3rds water. If every cell is 2/3 water what makes our cells different to water droplets. I'm going to suggest, intelligence and energy to keep this section short. Gerald proved our cells store energy and sunlight recharges the EZ component of water held in our cells. Our bodies work like rechargeable batteries.

Wow! They have fooled us again by suggesting we need protection from the sun, by smothering ourselves with toxic sunscreen that creeps into our cells, causing a toxic reaction over time. Sunlight energises our cells like a battery, which supports our electromagnetic systems to function optimally.

Gerald didn't explain why water provides pain relief but I know from experience that is the case. Prior to moving to the country, I was losing function from exposure to environmental EMR that I couldn't control. We had a swimming pool and for about six months of the year I would swim every day to get relief from pain, caused by inflammation and swelling in my body. In winter I would put my feet into the pool before I went to bed to relieve pain and reduce the buildup of negative energy in by body. Even today, if I'm feeling effects from EMF, I'll soak my feet in a basin of water and often add Epsom salts/magnesium salts to aid recovery. Do not underestimate how much power water has to help you heal.

**To be smarter than your smart phone, get a daily dose of sunshine:** Thirty minutes as the sun rises, thirty minutes in the middle of the day and thirty minutes around sunset. Blue light through the middle of the day is normal, orange light at dusk and firelight at night is normal, and even calming. The sun's rays re-charge you and help regulate your circadian rhythm. Your circadian rhythm is like a tuning fork for life. That juicy morsel of intel came from Dr. Jack Kruse, a neuro surgeon that changed his thinking to save his life. He calls it brain surgery without a scalpel.

**My last tip comes from Dr. Masaru Emoto**, previous chief of the Hado institute in Tokyo, Japan. Hado (pronounced hadou, which rhymes with shadow), means *wave* and *move*. Waves and moves relate to frequencies and changes, and it was Dr. Emoto's phenomenal discoveries of beautiful patterns of frozen water crystals, under high magnification, that led to his remarkable discovery that words are vibrations that influence water, positively and negatively. Quote from Office Masaru Emoto website. [109]

*"Hado: The intrinsic vibrational pattern at the atomic level in all matter. The smallest unit of energy. Its basis is the energy of human consciousness."*

*"Hado creates words. Words are the vibrations of nature. Therefore, beautiful words create beautiful nature. Ugly words create ugly nature. This is the root of the universe"* ~ **Masaru Emoto**

Be very careful of your thoughts and words. What you say to yourself and others can be harmful or helpful. Emoto recognised words are vibrations which are frequencies of energy. We can alter our environment and ourselves, positively and negatively by what we say. That alone is an amazing thought.

This phenomenon may be exactly what Albert Einstein was alluding to when he said,

> *"Influence the energy positively or negatively and that will be the result."*

This statement could also mean wireless frequencies and millimetre waves, i.e. environmental energy - which are vibrations, frequencies and energy - may be influenced, altered or changed - for good or bad – not only by man-made frequencies but by our thoughts too. This is where fear mongering (false evidence appearing as real) takes on a whole new perspective

Einstein also said, *"Everything is energy and that is all there is. Match the frequency of the reality you want and you cannot help but get that reality. It can be no other way. This is not philosophy. This is physics."*

**Has the truth been staring us in the face all this time?** Do Einstein's statements mean Profits @ Any Cost have known all along man-made energy, and specifically radio frequencies packed with data and information, have the ability to harm us and control us at the same time? Maybe they knew all along the world was waking up. This may have initiated a slow release of frequencies, from 1st, 2nd, 3rd, 4th and 5th generations of technology. Increasing the frequences, and volume of frequencies, over many years may have been intentional so we would be less likely to comprehend the reality of what was happening. Without canaries feeling these frequencies and alerting humanity to the harm they cause, we would likely not be aware of the damage to life on Earth. Maybe canaries caused a glitch in their plan, which explains why not many people know EMF canaries exist. Truth has been squashed and buried by enormous amounts of money invested in the media, medical system, education system and potential bribery of government officials and politicians. Has their intention always been to make money, and control what we think, and what we do? Let's investigate further to see if that theory could possibly be true.

Another road I ventured down suggests I am not wrong. This story highlights my earlier research, regarding the manufacture of disease and the treatments they unjustly dish out. It's a true story about a legendary discovery by Royal Raymond Rife [110] born in Elkhorn, Nebraska USA on May 16, 1888. Rife was an extraordinary scientist and inventor. In his early life he was presented with multiple awards for his research. In 1914 he received an honorary Doctor of Parasitology from the Heidelberg University in Germany, for creating an Atlas of Parasites, and he received an honorary Doctor of Science degree from the University of California in 1936 for his research into microscopy and cancer research. Rife was meticulous in his research of parasites and viruses, identifying individual frequencies, known as a signature for each microbe. He invented the world's first virus microscope. His microscope was unique in that it reached 60,000 times magnification. He developed a way to identify organisms and their frequency of vibration, known as the Mortal Oscillatory Rates (MOR's). Rife identified how a microbe and a virus have the ability to change from one form to another depending upon the medium they are in. Rife was able to successfully isolate a virus specific to cancer, due to its distinctive colour. He named it the BX virus (Bacillus X) which he identified in every instance of carcinoma he examined. He did hundreds of experiments which resulted in finding each microbe and each virus was susceptible to a certain frequency. With this knowledge he developed a machine to emit specific frequencies programmed to kill these microscopic organisms and named it the Rife Ray Tube system; a therapy for treatment of cancer. He treated sixteen terminally ill patients, brought to him in California from a hospital in San Diego. Fourteen of the patients were declared cancer free after ninety days. The other two patients continued treatment and were cancer free a month later.

At first Rife's treatment was heralded as the greatest medical discovery ever and he was invited to address the royal Society of Medicine in London.

Doctors and scientists praised his finding, with the Smithsonian Institute publishing an article in 1944. Once the American Medical Association (AMA) became aware of Rife's treatment, everything changed. Prominent doctors were paid to be silent. Most doctors continued to prescribe drugs, instead of recommending Rife's treatment method. During this period Rife's research was stolen and his associates laboratory mysteriously burned down. He was ostracised from the medical and scientific community. Medical journals failed to support Rife therapy, and AMA trained medical students graduated without knowledge of Rife's miracle treatment. Drugs and surgery were the only methods used to treat cancer at the time. During this period there was incredible growth of the American Cancer Society. Cancer charities, all funded by wealthy elites, popped up all around the world. Not one of them aware of the Rife technology that treats cancer without pain or side-effects. Instead, they invested millions of dollars into cancer treatments that neither cured cancer or made patients healthier, instead they literally killed them with medicine and unnecessary surgery. The AMA committed the biggest crime in living history, and they still get away with it. One in three people were predicted to get cancer in 1971, the year Royal Raymond Rife died, a broken man, due to the treatment dished out by Profits @ Any Cost. According to predictions, there will be over 35 million new cases of cancer by 2050, a 77% increase from an estimated 20 million in 2022. [111] Yikes!

In summary, surviving in today's world is not about fitting into the paradigm of profit, it's about being smarter than Profits @ Any Cost, and smarter than your smart phone. Taking necessary steps to reduce or eliminate the multitude of environmental toxins, firstly in your home because that's where you sleep and rejuvenate, and secondly in your workplace, where long-term exposure increases your risk of bio-accumulation. Too much EMF and too many toxins can deplete vital life force energy even in healthy individuals over time.

When travelling in a plane a Flight Attendants primary responsibility is the safety of passengers, and they always state - you must put your mask on first before helping your children or anyone else. This is an apt moment to recognise you can't help anyone else if you become incapacitated, indicating the need to take responsibility for your own health as a priority, to ensure you are able to look after others you love. Thinking this way could have great implications as we head into the most amazing time in living history, the Age of Aquarius. [112] It may be that the Universe has been hatching a plan that's identified in the stars. Astrolis.com [113] explains what the Age of Aquarius is and what is predicted:

> The Age of Aquarius isn't just a catchy phrase from a '60s song! It's an astrological era that's set to shake things up on a global scale. Rooted in the slow, cosmic dance of Earth's axis, the Age of Aquarius marks a shift in the collective energy of the world, influencing everything from technology to social structures. This change is part of a cycle called the precession of the equinoxes, where the Earth's wobble causes the Spring Equinox to move backward through the zodiac signs. Each age lasts about 2,160 years, and now, we're moving out of the Age of Pisces and into something entirely different…Aquarian energy pushes us to rethink how we live, work, and connect in a rapidly evolving world.

We have come a long way from Stage 1; the unconscious incompetence level of learning to an elevated state at Stage 2; conscious incompetence. Upskilling elevated us to Stage 3; conscious competence, to build a solid foundation from which to create a new paradigm on Earth.

More insights to get more life out of life are revealed in Chapter 4 and 5. Don't be discouraged, you're well on your way to being unconsciously competent, and masterfully capable of contributing to a new future where love, unity and consciousness play a major role.

# CHAPTER 4

# SOLUTIONS TO PROFITS
# @ ANY COST

*"When we are no longer able to change a situation,*
*we are challenged to change ourselves"*

- Viktor Frankl, author of Man's Search for Meaning

## MASTERING YOUR MIND VS MIND CONTROL

Sometimes solutions are wrapped up in obscure packaging. Here we'll explore not-so-obvious solutions to problems people rarely recognise they have.

### Overcoming a lack of seeing also called a blind spot.

Blind Spot; Hidden Biases of Good People, [114] a book by psychologist's Mahzarin Banaji and Anthony Greenwald exposes the concealed biases we all carry from a lifetime of learning and earning that trip us up and shape our judgements and our perceptions. Elizabeth Loftus PhD, wrote in her review of the book; *mental processes that we are not aware of can affect what we think and what we do.* David Myers, Professor from Hope College, suggests this book helps us think smarter and more humanely.

If we have unconscious biases, conscious biases and a multitude of influencing biases how can we make informed decisions or rely on others to make decisions in our favour when their biases influence their thinking, their reactions and their intentions, towards a result that might or might not be good for us. Let's unscramble this bias conundrum a little, to ensure you have an inkling about how the mind works and how it doesn't. If biases are kept in the dark, we are none the wiser.

A **confirmation bias** is the tendency to listen to information that confirms our existing belief. It's a bias that reinforces what we tend to believe because it appears to work in our favour. To overcome confirmation bias you need to listen to opposing arguments, question the research to see if it's reliable and open your mind to learning what the opposition has to say. Consider all the facts by willingly opening your mind to what is presented, so you know more about a subject, a person or a problem, especially the problem you need to solve.

An **anchoring bias** is a tendency to be mainly influenced by the first piece of information presented. Doctors can be susceptible to an anchoring bias when diagnosing patients. Often because of a first impression or in collaboration with an unconscious bias (they don't know they have), stopping them from carrying out a correct diagnosis.

An **unconscious bias** also known as an implicit bias is a form of discrimination and stereotyping, based on ability (or lack of), age, gender, race, education and experience or lack of experience, based on what you think you know, compared to what you need to know. When anyone with authority holds an unconscious bias, the results can be devastating to the individual that gets snookered by it.

**Cognitive bias** is similar but different. It differs because there is a predictable pattern of mental errors that result in an individual mis-perceiving reality. In reality what we see as best for us is hindered by what we want to believe is good for us.

**Are biases good or bad?** According to Matt Grawitch PhD, [115] Psychology Today, bias has acquired a slightly derogatory definition, as defined in the Merrian-Webster dictionary current definition: *an inclination of temperament or outlook; a personal and sometimes unreasoned judgement: A PREJUDICE.* In 1873 Herbert Spener remarked that biases can influence our beliefs much more so than evidence; it wouldn't be accurate to conclude that biases themselves are bad. They simply represent a predisposition to favour a given conclusion over other conclusions.

Grawitch states, *"some biases are hardwired into us through evolution. Other biases are learned; some are more generic and some based-on experiences."* Sometimes a bias can work in our favour or against us; when we choose fish and chips for instance, our bias is to ignore health advice. Or over time, middle age spread kicks in, when once we would have chosen pizza, we choose salad instead, believing it will stop the spread.

We have only scratched the surface of biases, which doesn't actually solve the bias problem, although now you know biases exist in many forms and there are many more that I haven't exposed, you may now be able to identify a bias when it hits you in the head, or you get a gut reaction, from a friend's biased reaction. Biases can be an indication of a learned behaviour, a habit: or a lack of learning, because you think you know; or it indicates a blind spot is stopping you or them, from seeing what's hidden behind a veil of misinformation.

We need to look at another form of mind management or lack thereof called cognitive dissonance. Dissonance means the opposite of harmony, of being out of tune or out of sync. Cognitive means, relating to the process of acquiring knowledge and understanding through thought, experience and the senses. Cognition is the process of knowing. Cognitive dissonance means our thinking is out of harmony, or we are in conflict with our thinking. Cognitive dissonance is alive and well in the world today. An example is when a smoker knows cigarette smoke can cause cancer but continues to smoke because the urge is more powerful than the will to stop. There are many other examples, however this one highlights the way our brain is tricked into doing something we instinctively know is bad because the pain of giving up something overwhelms the ability to think logically; disabling the individual from choosing an option that's in their best interests. Bad habits are very hard to break, especially when linked to addictions like alcohol or drugs. Gambling habits can be disastrous, especially when people get hooked after getting a win. These habits are linked to operant conditioning, something you'll learn about shortly.

Real life examples of cognitive dissonance are at play every day. Here's an example: George is the last person standing out of six people living in three co-joined units. George continually prompted Joan, his wife to be cautious with technology and he warned her about using talcum powder, but to no avail. Joan was diagnosed with lung cancer which went to her brain, killing her. Between 2015-2019, Joan and three occupants of the units on either side of George died of cancer and another person died from an aneurism. It didn't matter how many times George expressed his concern and highlighted the risks of wireless radiation and talc; the message never got through. Could these deaths be related to a 5G phone tower installed near the property in 2015? George thinks so, because that's when his health started to deteriorate.

Another very sad and true story of how cognitive dissonance works, comes from Tasmania. I met with my real estate agent in 2019 to find a tenant for a property. As I sat in his office, I could see a phone tower on a building across the street. I suggested it was a problem, and he should not spend time in this location. He was not concerned, because he spent more time working from home, and he handled the property and the electricity account for the building. It was a money-making, five-story building with shops on the ground floor. None of the offices above were tenanted anymore, but the rent from hosting the telephone tower was more than enough income to compensate for vacant offices. What was even more amazing - the electricity bill to run the telephone tower was greater than the tenancy income of the whole building. The story doesn't stop there. When I asked if he had any health issues, and he said he suffered from severe eczema and was on medication to control it. His doctor told him it would shorten his life because of the side-effects, but he said *"life without it was unbearable."* I also inquired about his home and what technology he used. He was an avid user of Wi-Fi for everything; from his smart TV to his computer and he was continually on his mobile phone. I suggested he switch to wired internet and work mainly from a landline. He wasn't concerned in fact he totally rejected my information.

Early in 2024 I tried contacting him to find another tenant, and he was not available. After I left a message, his boss phoned me and said he had recently passed from a rare stomach cancer that grew in the lining around his stomach. Over the last twelve months Brenden (not his real name) had gone from mildly affected to not being able to move or talk and eventually he couldn't eat or function at all. It was an excruciatingly slow death. Death by cognitive dissonance is similar to death by, "it's not my problem." I'll explain shortly.

I had a dose of cognitive dissonance when I first started to feel the effects of wireless radiation. It wasn't until I got hit with the sledge hammer that I took decisive action, and exited suburbia; a move that changed everything. Exposing biases and cognitive dissonance is aimed at helping you understand how difficult it is to make an informed decision when you have two very powerful mind controlling influences working against you. Mind control needs to be explored not ignored. If we are to be controllers of our destiny and defenders of our kingdom. We need to be masters of our mind and our environment.

## INFLUENCE – FRIEND OR FOE

During marketing training, Eben Pagan suggested reading, INFLUENCE, a book by Robert Cialdini, about the psychology of persuasion. [116] I absolutely loved this book. It explains many things we are not aware of, for example; if people hear a story about someone taking their own life, then suicide by whatever means, increases deaths by suicide by an alarming amount. It's the reason why suicide, and how the person died, is not reported in the media.

In a section called CAUSE OF DEATH: UNCERTAIN(TY), Cialdini states, *"in general, when we are unsure of ourselves, when the situation is unclear or ambiguous, when uncertainty reigns, we are most likely to look to, and accept the actions of others."* This led to a fascinating phenomenon called *pluralistic ignorance.* A tendency to look at what everyone else is doing, classified as social evidence. To explain, he mentioned a murder of a woman in her late twenties in Queens, New York City. Catherine Genovese was walking home from work when she was attacked and murdered. It wasn't a quick affair, Catherine was not killed instantly, she was chased for thirty-five minutes, attacked three times as she screamed and cried out for help, while thirty-eight people looked on before her attacker finally ended her cries for help with a knife. Her neighbours observed the incident from the safety of their apartments, believing someone else would help, hence they did nothing. No one called the police during the attack and only one person called after she was dead. Catherine died because "good people" did nothing.

This case was examined by police, and the media. TV stations became involved in the story and it appeared, after much scrutiny and investigation, the onlookers were normal people that hadn't cared enough to get involved. The evidence was in. Quote: *"we were becoming a nation of selfish, insensitive people…and indifferent to the plight of our fellow citizens."* The second reasoning involved the pluralistic ignorance effect, which explains, when an emergency is often not seen as an emergency, it is ignored. This could also be explained by social engineering; people conditioned by TV violence, weaponised video games and mainstream news, adopt the attitude "it's not my problem."

Have we been conditioned to NOT care?

Another experiment I read about, based on conditioning, involved putting a dog in a box with high sides. The dog was given a small electric shock through the bottom of the box. At first the dog would whelp and try to jump out of the box, but couldn't. Over time the dog accepted the shocks and did not respond. When another dog was put in the box and the sides were lowered, enough to jump out, the dog that wasn't conditioned by electric shocks would immediately jump out when the electric shock was applied. The conditioned dog didn't attempt to jump out, it was conditioned to accept the pain as normal and didn't try to escape. When an individual or a group is subject to adverse stimulus, neuroscience has provided insight into learned helplessness. An individual's belief in a lack of ability to achieve a goal is said to contribute to learned helplessness. Additionally, mental illness, as an outcome of learned helplessness may result in a perceived absence of control over the outcome of a situation. Reference: research by Martin Seligman, on learned helplessness 1967. [117]

Have we been conditioned to accept biological effects from RFR as a natural part of life or that headaches, inflammation, and childhood autism is normal? Have we been lulled into a false sense of security because research offers small glimmers of hope when scientists expose the truth, but no one actually does anything about it? Are those affected by wireless radiation, the lucky ones that find their safe place or are they the unlucky ones that suffer the belief "it's not my problem," or "it's your problem, I'm ok." I believe it's both.

*"All that is necessary for the triumph of evil is that good men do nothing."* ~ British statesman, Edmund Burke.

## PSYCHOLOGICAL EXPERIMENTS REVEALED

To get my head around this *conditioning* thing, that appears to have happened to people all around the world for many years, or at least the last seventy years, I read Opening Skinner's Box, [118] a book recommended to me by Riccardo Bosi, head of Australia One, [119] (Bosi provides an alternative to our current political system). Author Lauren Slater explores great psychological experiments of the twentieth century. B. F. Skinner was born in 1904 and died in 1990. He was America's leading neo-behaviorist, known for his famous animal experiments to shape learned behaviour. Skinner hugely influenced operant conditioning, where humans used positive reinforcement to train dogs and humans to function on commands.

One of Skinner's experiments was on rats that were conditioned to press a lever to access food, the reward. Over time he discovered he could condition the rats to press the lever multiple times without a reward. As long as a reward was given intermittently, they would continue to press the lever. The ultimate discovery was that irregular rewarded behaviour was the hardest of all to eradicate. This has huge implications for just about everything created for profit. It explains why people get addicted to gambling, because they get intermittent rewards, and are conditioned to keep pressing the buttons, expecting a win.

This conditioning can be found in politics, video gaming and likely in situations where people keep looking for a reward, once they get a taste of what they are after, they want more. In doctors' surgeries, where people go for treatment and some treatment works, convincing them doctors heal, they continue going back, even though they never really get better. Could there be a multitude of mind controlling beliefs going on every day, controlling our minds that we are not aware of. Social media, controlled Google algorithms and everyday news articles come to mind. Could these rarely exposed experiments be linked to mental conditioning through education and indoctrination by Profits @ Any Cost? Hmm!

Could this conditioning be part of the grand plan to control us and influence choices, most of us would not make if we knew the truth?

## Education or indoctrination

A standard education is a system based on doing what you're told, what to think, and not to step out of line. Instead of an education that teaches you how to think for yourself or use your intuition to identify cause-and-effect scenarios. In nature no animal, insect or plant does what it's told; it relies on natural intelligence, instinct, and its connection to magnetism and natural frequencies. That's how birds for example, navigate from the Northern hemisphere to the Southern hemisphere; to return to their nest or nesting place year after year to breed. Homing pigeons and whales don't use maps; they use their senses and Earth's magnetic field as a guide. Could the beaching of whales be linked to man-made frequencies, or sonar, that distorts the whales' ability to detect the natural frequencies, driving them off course? Nature gives us clues if we pay attention, so do results.

Natural unadulterated food holds intelligence and life force energy, and our cells use life force energy when we need it, as detailed in the fourth phase of water. Seeds contain natural intelligence, sufficient to grow into a plant, that forms more seeds, to produce more life. Our cells know what to do, it's our education that's stuffed things up. If we didn't have natural intelligence our body wouldn't heal. If food doesn't go mouldy it contains something to keep it from naturally decaying. Food that sits on a shelf for six months is not full of intelligence, it's full of preservatives and artificial ingredients, which is not designed to sustain life but to sustain a profit. All food contains information based on the integrity of the energy it contains. Sources of good energy and intelligence will repair and rejuvenate. Unnatural or toxic food produces inflammation and disharmony in the body. One example is coeliac disease; scientifically linked to Roundup Ready wheat, engineered through genetically modifying an organism (GMO). Children's Health Defence have been fighting for human rights for a long time and provide eye opening conversations with leading health experts, exposing the monstruous power of chemical companies. [120] GMO crops are not designed for people, they are designed to make a profit and to control the agricultural industry for the benefit of Profits @ Any Cost. Stephanie Seneff PhD, is a Glyphosate expert, warning the world of its long-lasting toxicity. [121] Critical information is provided by Stephanie Seneff in TOXIC LEGACY; How the Weedkiller GLYSOPHATE is Destroying Our Health and the Environment. Robert F. Kennedy Jr., US attorney, founder and Chief Legal Counsel for Children's Health Defence has been fighting Monsanto (now Bayer) for years, exposing how their products have been harming people and the environment. Glyphosate, sprayed on more than 70 different crops including canola, soy, corn and wheat, is linked to non-Hodgkin lymphoma, colon cancer, kidney cancer, coeliac disease, neuroinflammation, mitochondrial dysfunction and more.

You can listen to an interview with RFK Jr. explaining how they get away with it on YouTube. [122]

## Placebo v Nocebo

Scientists and doctors are aware of the placebo effect, when, during drug trials, half the test patients are given sugar pills and the other half are given the trial drug. Often people taking the sugar pill get better, not because the sugar pill worked but because they believed the drug would help them. Most people don't know is there's an opposite effect to the placebo (a positive effect), called a nocebo effect, (a negative effect), where, if the patient is told their condition is incurable, they believe it and their body accommodates that belief. Stories in the Biology of Belief by Dr. Bruce Lipton, [123] explained how people were cured because the placebo effect was stronger than the nocebo effect. Tragically a train guard, that accidently locked himself inside a refrigerated train carriage overnight, died unnecessarily. When he realised he couldn't get out, he recorded his last hours; writing down how he was getting colder and colder as the night progressed, and was found dead in the morning. He didn't die of exposure, because the refrigeration system was broken and not working, and the temperature didn't get below 5° Celsius. He died because he believed he was going to die. That's how powerful the nocebo effect is.

How important is the placebo effect? This story explains it very well; I met a guy, we'll call him Chris, at an event in Federation Square, Melbourne, where we, a group of Building Biologists, set up a marquee to provide information to the public about Building Biology, and the skills and services we offered. Chris came up to me wanting information about mould and I told him what I knew. He was happy with that, but then explained he was a physicist and had recovered from an extremely rare blood disease similar to leukemia. He was treated by a doctor in the UK and after treatment he recovered. Chris was a pretty cluey guy who'd conducted his own research as to why he developed this rare condition. He put it down to living in a mouldy building and he moved out, which may have contributed to his recovery. His wife was a Chinese medicine practitioner, which could have contributed to his recovery, but he totally believed his positive mindset, enabled him to recover. Only when he was given the all clear five years after diagnosis, did his treating doctor tell him no one had ever survived the treatment. He absolutely believed the placebo effect saved his life.

I'm a great believer the placebo affect works but to give it oomph I listen to my gut and my body, because it has the intelligence you need and your body doesn't tell lies. I suggest reading, *Your Body Doesn't Lie,* by John Diamond, M.D., [124] to gain more insights into how the body knows. This book about Behavioural Kinesiology, explains how muscle testing, using a partner or a professional, to determine what the body needs or what is toxic, helps with a diagnosis. Useful for anybody wanting to improve health outcomes or physicians that genuinely want their patients to recover. Behavioural Kinesiology uses the body's intelligence, based on Applied Kinesiology techniques. Dr. Diamond explains how a person's surroundings and life-style can raise or lower bodily energy. Sugar can have a negative effect, as can modern technology. Diamond stated, *"all illness starts with a decrease of Life Energy of the body".* The thymus gland, located in the chest, between the lungs, behind the breast bone, is a small important gland that's part of the lymphatic system. It makes white blood cells, an especially important immune response to fight disease and infection. Its role is that of immunological surveillance, like a soldier on the inside of you, detecting aliens or friends and deploying T-cells to beat the aliens (cancer causing agents). The thymus is the first organ in the body to be affected by stress, and an emotional state of mind. It is in fact an important link between mind and body. I loved this book and couldn't believe it answered so many questions, as to why anger and fear are precursors to disease, and why love, trust, and gratitude are good for you. Emotional states that weaken the body include hate, envy and fear while emotional states of love, happiness, joy and positivity strengthen the body. Wow! The things you learn when you delve into natural healing and alternative therapies.

## PATH TO ENLIGHTENMENT

Detective work takes time and sometimes clues lead you up the wrong path to dead ends and sometimes to surprises. We are well on the way to unearthing the mysteries of the world and why Profits @ Any Cost will do anything to keep us from knowing the truth.

You may not have realized you're on a path to enlightenment, because the evidence points to doom and gloom, but what if we're on the edge of a new beginning. Would you be willing to change your thinking to get a different result. Keeping a positive mindset might be all that's needed. According to Einstein; doing the same thing over and over again and expecting a different outcome, is insanity. So why do we think governments or telcos will change RF radiation to make it safe, or that Profits @ Any cost will willingly let us gain control. It's time to think differently, especially about solutions.

My path to enlightenment gained a greater level of awareness when I read multiple books by Peter Dingle PhD. I was introduced to Peter by friends in Queensland and attended his information sessions on health, nutrition and how we are misled about drugs and the medical system. I purchased multiples of Peter's books to improve my clients' knowledge, and sometimes gave them away for free with a consult, because at that time I focused on Wellness Inspired Construction, Knowledge & Environmental Design - a WICKED idea using the science of Building Biology and solar passive design, and wasn't focused on writing a book. Peter was the former Associate Professor in Nutritional and Environmental Toxicology at Murdoch University in Western Australia. He was a well-recognised educator on environmental and nutritional toxicology and heralded as a true healthy life advocate. It was his book *Modern Myths & Health Lies That are Killing Us* [125] that profoundly changed my belief about the medical system and the controlled manufacturing industry. Peter exposed how toxic ingredients in sunscreen have an effect at a cellar level, with epidemiological studies showing people who use sunscreens sold in supermarkets and pharmacies, increase their risk of getting skin cancer. He exposed the myth that modern medicine has extended our lives and many other myths about pharmaceuticals, toxic ingredients in manufactured food, makeup and personal care products sold as *good for you,* but in reality, are toxic to the body.

What most people wouldn't know, is how people in organisations with systems of control, including the education system, legal system, medical system and media, will attack you, vilify you, and ruin all your hard work if you tell a truth publicly, that exposes the hierarchy of control in some way. Peter's life was ruined after his first wife died of cancer, virtually blaming him for her death. You'd have to read his book to get the true version of what transpired, because what they post on Wikipedia, and in the press, is fabricated. In today's world, they shoot the messenger, or take down anyone who is a threat to the monopoly of control, like they did with Dr Andrew Wakefield in the UK, and Dr Charlie Teo a brain surgeon in Australia. Dr Robert O. Becker is another example of shooting the messenger. Becker was twice nominated for a Nobel Prize for his groundbreaking research on tissue regeneration. He discovered our bodies respond not only to chemicals but to electricity. Natural electrical processes in the body are severely disrupted by man-made EMF. In 1977 Becker made the fatal error of alerting the public to his discoveries. His studies included animal and human trials, where animals exposed to ELF showed signs of biological stress and slow growth rates. Humans exposed to ELF exhibited elevated blood lipids, indicating risk for cardiovascular disease. When he reported his findings on a 60 minutes interview his research was no longer funded and he became an inconvenient scientist. An article in The Economic Times [126] tells the story of how his funding vanished, as did his career in academic medicine, because he told the truth, and that was nearly fifty years ago. What we have here is a pattern repeat, where inconvenient knowledge shared becomes dangerous for those that share it. On that note, I am not suicidal, I am healthy and show no signs of a brain tumor or cancer. I've tested my body using the Kinesiology method I learned from Dr Diamond's book and from a friend, qualified in Applied Kinesiology. I'm planning on living a long life. Just so you know, in case something weird should happen.

## Progression; one step at a time

Mastering the four stages of learning may seem daunting for some but what if it was as simple as taking one step at a time, and there's only four steps, so what's holding you back? Moving from unconscious incompetence to conscious incompetence requires a spark to light the fire of learning or a need. Moving from conscious incompetence to **conscious competence** takes effort to gain a skill or increase learning. Progressing to **unconscious competence** takes practice and time. Here's an example of the different stages to help you gain clarity.

My first step to empowerment began when a friend convinced me to attend an aerobics class, to get my mojo (energy) back, about twelve months after I'd had our third son. Stage 1: I had no idea exercise to music would be a great self-improvement tool, physically, mentally and emotionally. Stage 2: Working out to music challenged me. I felt incompetent at first, because my body and mind had not been programmed to function this way. I was outside my comfort zone. Stage 3: After the initial learning phase, aerobics proved to be energising, fun and great for stress relief. Regular exercise changed my mind and body, and it made me feel great. After twelve months of attending aerobic classes and learning the basics, I wanted to learn more and signed up to the Institute of Fitness to become a fitness leader. Stage 4. After gaining my basic qualification, friends asked me to take classes in the local community hall. I loved it so much I didn't want to stop to have another baby, so I didn't. With help from my husband, we created a gym in a shed on our property to make it easier for me to hold classes, and to eliminate the need to cart equipment around. After one year I became pregnant, and continued taking aerobic and circuit training classes twice a day for five days a week, up to the day I gave birth to our fourth son, and within two weeks I was back taking classes again. During fitness training I learned how important it is to warm up muscles, before working out, how muscles stretch when they are warm (full of blood) but not when cold, how muscles have memory, and how important hydration is for performance. And with practice and repetition, performance improves over time. It doesn't matter if it's aerobic training (with oxygen to improve heart and lung capacity) or anaerobic weight training (without oxygen to build muscle power). Everyone benefits from having a coach to guide their improvement. This story is a metaphor for life. Where there's a will, there's a way.

Stage 4 takes practice to get better. Initially instructing aerobic classes in the early 90's, I would have to plan and practice my choreography well in advance before I took a class. I was constantly focused on developing my skills and after a few years, I could face my class, move left when I told them to move right, keep in time with the music, tell them in advance what step to do next and at the same time count repetitions and increase intensity based on how well everyone was keeping up. All this brain activity would happen automatically; in other words, I'd mastered the art of leading by developing unconscious competence. Each level of learning from stage 1 is a step up, to reach stage 4. Anyone can advance their learning level, but not without the will to achieve. Having someone lead or instruct in the early stages is critical. Once you learn how to learn, you can apply it to anything you do in life.

Evidence of this higher level of proficiency can be found in elite sports, music, business, and performing arts. Instinct takes over thinking and actions are automatic. For example, I've seen jazz musicians jam together, where, with no prior practice they instantly play in harmony with people they just met. Unconscious competence is more prevalent than you may realise.

Many people never get past unconscious incompetence - to learn how corrupt the pyramid of power truly is. Canaries are the evidence this corruption exists and learning how their lives are affected in every way is heartbreaking. I'm one of the lucky ones, able to take control of my environment, mostly because I took control of my thinking when I gained an alternate education. Do not underestimate how powerful an alternative education is. It literally saved my life and I couldn't be more grateful to the people providing this education and to the wonderful people enlightening me about the great deception within the systems that control us. When I discovered we were going through the Greatest Awakening of all time, I was thrilled, believing all would be revealed after the covid fiasco. When that didn't happen, from a mainstream news perspective, I realised it may be a long time before we develop harmonised thinking. For those still at the unconscious incompetence level, it may take a gigantic reveal of some kind to nudge them into action, or at least make them curious enough to listen to people shining light on the truth. Unfortunately, some may hold onto their normal (controlling) education because it's too difficult to believe anything different.

In summary, mastering your mind and seeing clearly to make wise decisions can be a bit tricky due to a whole lot of habits and unintentional learned helplessness (or intentional as the case may be). It appears good people are conditioned to believe, *"it's not my problem"* leading to most doing nothing when a life is in danger. Detective work is not easy, and it can lead to dead ends. Pun intended. It's obvious anyone exposing the truth becomes a target, because the truth is not what Profits @ Any Cost and DS operatives want you to know. It is time to wake up to the monopoly of power and do things differently. Top-down conditioning, attached to money-making ventures, and reliance on systems that fail us, could be our ultimate demise. However, here's the good news, if more people develop conscious competence, that leads to unconscious competence, especially in the areas of bull shit (BS) detection, EMF/RFR detection, and greater awareness of our supernatural talents, we could turn things around. With that thought in mind, let's continue on the path to enlightenment, because seeking a good ending is the aim of the game of life, and I for one, am not happy to roll over and play the deaf, dumb and blind game, ever.

# CHAPTER 5

# CHANGING THE PARADIGM
# OF PROFIT

*"If you are not willing to learn, no one can help you. If
you are determined to learn, no one can stop you."*

- Zig Ziglar

## IDENTIFYING FALSE NARRATIVES TO FIND
## REAL SOLUTIONS

Wikipedia is used by many to find information, me included. Trouble is Wikipedia provides a false narrative when truth doesn't suit Profits @ Any Cost. Look up BioInitiative Report on Wikipedia and you'll find a fabricated perception of the science of EMF. They use trick-you-tactics all the time. When you investigate the science conducted and paid for by the Deep State, you will find no evidence of harm, when in fact, not one honest scientist would say microwaves are safe. When you know the truth, it's easy to detect lies in plain sight. Once you see clearly, you are no longer fooled by false narratives.

Being a detective requires you to ask different questions and build a different perception, which is a picture in your mind. Once you've been bitten by the dog (mechanism of lies) you are less likely to trust the dogs that bit you. If everything on Wikipedia was a lie, it wouldn't be trusted. That's why sometimes I like Wikipedia, because it does provide clarification on some subjects. This is where discernment; the ability to decipher fact from fiction, is necessary. Practicing discernment comes in handy if you wish to reach the unconscious competence level of learning. One of the things I uncovered was the pattern of thinking - a paradigm, that took away our common sense and replaced it with dogma, which is an opinion or a doctrine that is often established by an assertion - without evidence – that is commonly repeated until it appears as truth. In other words, lies spread often enough, end up being believed to be true.

Wikipedia's explanation of a paradigm, is not bad, so let's use it:

> *In science and philosophy, a paradigm is a distinct set of concepts or thought patterns, including theories, research methods, postulates and standards for what constitute legitimate contributions to a field. The word paradigm is Greek in origin, meaning "pattern".*[127]

Did anything in that statement indicate there was truth to a paradigm. No, because a paradigm can be created out of thin air, or created because it serves a purpose, through education, through parental influences or an experience. I first learnt about paradigms from reading Stephen Covey's book *7 Habits of Highly Effective People*.[128] A great read, but can be challenging for anyone not willing to give up what's holding them back. Covey gets you to investigate the paradigm of you. He challenges you to understand why you think what you think and if what you think serves you well. I was so into his theories I bought his CD's and listened to them over and over in the car to master the 7 Habits. That said. I'd better get back on track and continue to explain how the paradigm of profit holds you under a spell.

We've exposed the pattern of deception used by world health authorities, governments and the telecommunications and technology industry. When you become aware of the paradigm of deception you can detect misinformation, fake news and easily see how the paid for, news media and public relations industry manipulate your mind and your thinking. Advertising, science, politics, education curriculum have all been manipulated to ensure people are blind to truth. Social media has taken brain washing to another level. Not only does the main stream news fail to report the facts, social media bans you from telling the truth and AI keeps posts away from unsuspecting people, because real truth comes with a price tag. If you want to learn the truth you actually have to buy a book, subscribe to a channel or use alternative education to dodge the dogma perpetrated by the manipulators. You have to write a book, like this one, or set-up an alternative news channel and get people to subscribe to help pay the costs of running it. Nothing is free, not even the truth.

Once you unhook from the matrix and do your own research, you develop a sixth sense. I call it the bullshit (BS) detector, that kicks in every time you read something or hear something in the media that makes no sense at all, and you recognise brainwashing is the glue holding people in the matrix or, what's simply holding the baloney together. As more and more people gain this sixth sense, the BS holding patterns of the matrix become weaker and weaker, to the extent the belief in the systems erode. With a concerted effort these beliefs might actually fall apart one day, so let's prepare for that day.

You are now at the turning point where you can reject the evidence of the problems we face, or embrace the knowledge you have gained, and select a new paradigm to be sustainable in every way. Here's a guide post for you.

## BLUE ZONES; WHAT THEY DON'T TELL YOU

When searching for clues to live a long and healthy life I came across Blue Zones; places in the world **where people live the longest with less illness and disease**. Dan Beuttner from National Geographic identified what people in Blue Zones do to live remarkably well and wrote a book; *The Blue Zones: Lessons for living longer from the people who've lived the longest.* There are five places around the world Beuttner visited and wrote about: Okinawa in Japan; pockets of people in Sardinia, Italy; Loma Linda, a Seventh Day Adventist community in California; Nicoya, Costa Rica;

and the most recent addition Ikaria, a Greek island in the Aegean Sea, all visited by Beuttner. [129]

My best mate and I joined a group of wellness enthusiasts, to experience what a Blue Zone had to offer. The trip to Ikaria was arranged by 100 Not Out Podcasters, Dr Damian Kristoff and Marcus Pearce in 2016. Here I expose what Dan Beuttner did not reveal in his book, which I believe is very telling.

**The first insight; the community self-regulate.** They do not rely on the government or police to enforce laws; they have their own unwritten laws, and people in the community step in to sort things out when individuals go off the rails. They self-manage, take responsibility and have an understood tolerance level. In other words, they don't tolerate bad behaviour.

**Insight number two** was revealed when we went to a Panigiri, a village festival, held to raise money for the village church. Ikarians are very protective of their people and their community. They don't like outsiders. According to Thea our host; focus on the Blue Zone phenomenon is having a negative effect on their belief about longevity, something they don't usually think about. This does not mean they are inhospitable; they are the friendliest and most welcoming people however, focusing on the elderly and longevity does not sit well with them, mainly because it's not what they focus on. **Protecting their community is extremely important – we were outsiders** and a bit of a pain in the neck to some, or so it seemed.

**Insight number three; their world is changing,** not just because life on Ikaria is broadcast around the world now as one of the longest-lived communities but because they have Wi-Fi and use it daily. Telephone transmitting wireless towers have been placed on hills high above the villages and everyone is connected. This may prove to be the biggest problem and not the influx of visitors in the future.

**Insight four; all generations are happy to live together,** if necessary, party together, work together, share responsibility and respect what each has to offer. There is no segregation of the elderly into aged care facilities or the too hard to deal with basket. They work it out and look after their own. As Dan says, *"invest time and energy in your children, your spouse and your parents. Play with your children, nurture your marriage, and honour your parents."*

**Family** was identified as extremely important in all Blue Zones and Ikaria is no exception. Money is not the highest priority, their relationships with all generations stood out as being a blessing for all. As Thea, our host explained, the young people respect the eldest people and the older generation listen to the young people. **Everyone contributes and everyone matters.**

**Purpose** is important in all Blue Zones. Everyone has a purpose to fulfill in Ikaria. It could be the vegetables they produce, the family they take care of, the business they run, the wine they make or the community they support. Everyone has something to contribute.

**Insight five; Ikarians' do not stress,** they have a relaxed disposition and an accepting outlook. On first sight we were amazed at how inhospitable the terrain of Ikaria was. The landscape is steep, rocky, and not easy to live with. We would not build where they build, we would not farm where they farm, we would not tolerate the lack of services or the lack of money. Ikarian people have learnt to live with less and stress less about what they can't have and can't do. The obvious was not obvious when we first travelled from the airport to Thea's Inn, they have to manage the best way they can, on their terms, and in their own way. The government doesn't contribute.

I asked Thea "who sets the rules or laws?" The answer, is the National Greek government however, because the government is what you might call insolvent (through corruption, one Greek lady told me) and because many difficulties need to be overcome (not just on the island of Ikaria), people are left to sort things out for themselves. The government taxes new homes and not the second or third home of Greek people. This fact may be why most young people cannot afford to build new homes; therefore, most new homes are being built by wealthy people from other countries. This means it is more beneficial for a family to extend their home, than to initiate a new build. **They get around the problems by valuing things differently.**

**Insight six; they make their own rules** around the laws that govern them. An example; people park where no parking signs are erected. People make allowances because the streets are tight and narrow that weave through the villages and because parking is limited, they make adjustments. Another was the way Thea cares about her employees. They are like family and in Ikaria they look after Thea, and Thea looks after them, so everyone wins. It does not help anyone live better if the National laws are strictly adhered to. In other words, complying to the laws is less than beneficial. The only problem Thea alluded to, was the amount of paperwork to complete. It seems even on Ikaria; you can't dodge the paperwork.

**Insight seven; the amount of No's,** no chemical additives in the water, no industry, no traffic jams or congestion, no medical benefits, no one lined up for prescriptions, no adherence to strict safety laws, no seat belts, no motor cycle helmets, no laziness, no toilet paper down the toilet, because it clogs up the septic system and no or little crime. Everyone knows who you are and crime would not pay. People leave their cars unlocked just in case they need to be moved and no one cares if it's in the way, they'll just move it. Actually, there is **no stress** because everything gets fixed that needs to get fixed by the people, not the government.

There's very little mental illness or dementia and very low levels of cancer and heart disease and other inflammatory disease in the community, even later in life, which is not the norm in our society. It could be the olive oil, red wine, exercise, no pollution, happy people or less stress that helps or maybe they just lead a simple life and have less to worry about. Our society, is heading in the wrong direction; people as young as 30, 40 and 50 are being diagnosed with dementia in Australia, and 54% of people living in permanent aged care have dementia. More than 1.6 million people in Australia are involved in the care of someone living with dementia. Dementia is the leading cause of death for Australian women (Dementia Australia). [130] Something is amiss in our society.

**Insight eight: the older generation have never searched for a silver bullet**, they do not do gym classes, follow diets, pop pills, take supplements, hang out at the emergency ward or rely on government handouts because there are no handouts. They do not expect others to be their saviour, they use food as their medicine and love their life, they do not complain. There is no magic bullet on Ikaria, only a life lived well, on purpose, naturally and with those they love. Seems like a good recipe to me. This is prevention of illness and disease in action, they do not need someone to tell them how to live, they just do it their way, on their terms.

**Insight nine: time is not important** to Ikarian people. Time, in their world was the exact opposite of how time is regulated in our world. Most people do not punch a time clock, unless it's necessary, to catch a ferry or a plane. Time was rarely a focus, and the belief, time is money didn't exist. If that one thing could be changed, we would all be healthier and less stressed. Time is endless, there will always be a tomorrow and there is always time for the things you need to do. Ikarian people spend more time doing what they love on a regular basis. It appears, if you make time for the things you love, and do what is good for you, you will end up with more lifetime.

The ninth strategy in the Blue Zone book centres on the person you are. Evidently people that live the longest are likable and they have lots of friends or as Dan says *"likable old people are more likely to have a social network, frequent visitors and de facto caregivers. They seem to experience less stress and live purposeful lives."* **Building strong friendship takes some effort, and it seems a little effort goes a long way.**

When you begin to understand the secrets to sustainable health, well-being and longevity you realise our world is designed to keep us in fear (false evidence appearing as real) creating crisis after crisis, the war on terrorism, the war in Israel and all world wars. We are divided by religion, colour, race, rank, gender, political persuasion and division of the family unit. Not valuing women as mothers and home makers but valuing careers and gender equality (everyone needs an income to pay more tax), all for profit and control. Ikaria is a community that managers life, without a handout, by doing life their way.

**Ikaria Summary:** solutions to Profits @ Any Cost are not found in the systems that control us, they are found in people willing to make different choices to sustain life for many generations in the future.

## Sustainability of people and planet is not about climate change

Sustainability is not what you have been led to believe. It's not about stopping greenhouse gas emissions, energy efficiency ratings, and everyone driving electric vehicles. Climate change is a hoax. Climate View News founder Jim Lee has been separating fact from fiction since 2012. [131] Jim provides open-source news on geoengineering, and weather modification history. This is where conspiracy meets reality.

In my opinion, climate change is a money-making venture as well as a control mechanism linked to PROBLEM – REACTION - SOLUTION. Investigating climate change exposed what's really going on. It's another Profit @ Any Cost tactic to swindle money from unsuspecting people, it's not about sustainability of people or the planet. For sustainability of people and planet, everybody and every community needs to be sustainably healthy, free of disease and dis-stress and biologically, and ecologically in tune with nature.

*"When bad men combine, good men must organize."* ~ Edmund Burke.

## BUILDING BIOLOGY GETS THE TICK FOR LIFE-TIME SUSTAINABILITY

We're getting to the pointy end of the pyramid of human potential, where consciousness gets a competence upgrade. To know and not do, is not to know. Mastering the unconscious competence level of survival requires overcoming dysfunctional education systems and misrepresentation of the facts regarding sustainability. PROBLEM - REACTION - SOLUTION is a strategy to make billions of dollars by fooling the people, again and again. Once you're awake to their tactics, you can say "no more can the veil of deception be pulled over my eyes."

When you recognize PROBLEM – REACTION - SOLUTION every time it appears in front of you, on the mainstream news, or when a programmed scientist speaks, you're way ahead of the rest. This is a sign you've reached the unconscious competence level of learning. Let's continue.

Becoming master of your environment requires you to be master of your mind, which an alternate education aims to do. This is where it gets simpler, not harder. We've established RF/EMF, mould, chemicals and stress collide with our biological systems. Next step is easy. All we need to do is create an environment that sustains life. The science of building biology does more than that, it's aimed at reducing our environmental footprint; it's science that's good for people, planet and future generations.

Building Biology doesn't fix every problem, but it works in collaboration with nature, to do no harm. Similar to North American indigenous philosophy of the Seventh Generation Principal, [132] emphasizing decisions we make today, should result in a sustainable world seven generations into the future. Building Biology founders have already written the recipe for sustainable homes, which ensures a dwelling is life-enhancing for all its inhabitants, not detrimental to its builders, with as little disruption to the environment as possible. [133]

## 25 Guiding Principles to design and construct a truly sustainable home

### Site and Community Design

1.  Verify that the site is free of naturally-occurring and human-made health hazards.

2.  Place dwellings so occupants are undisturbed by sources of human-made environmental pollution including electro-pollution.

3.  Place dwellings in well-planned communities that provide ample access to fresh air, sunshine and nature.

4.  Plan homes and developments considering the needs of community, families and individuals of all ages.

**Electromagnetic Radiation Health**

5.  Provide an abundance of well-balanced natural light and safe illumination while using colour in accordance with nature.

6.  Minimize building material interference with natural terrestrial radiation and introduced electrification.

7.  Adopt appropriate strategies to minimize exposure to harmful electromagnetic radiation generated as a result of building electrification.

8.  Adopt appropriate avoidance and shielding strategies to minimize exposure to radio frequency radiation generated by wireless devices within the building and from wireless sources outside the building

9.  Avoid use of building materials that have elevated radioactivity levels.

**Indoor Air and Water Quality**

10. Assure low total moisture content and rapid drying of wet construction processes in new buildings.

11. Provide for ample ventilation.

12. All building materials shall be non-toxic with neutral or pleasant natural scents using natural and unadulterated building systems and materials.

13. Use appropriate water and moisture exclusion techniques to prevent internal moisture issues sufficient to support growth of fungi, bacteria and dust mites. Use established techniques to address water ingress, stormwater transportation and wastewater management.

14. Assure best possible water quality by applying purification technologies as required.

## Occupant Well-being

15. Allow natural self-regulation of indoor air humidity, sound attenuation and healthy ion balance using hygroscopic (humidity buffering) and sorbent materials and finishes.

16. Design for a climatically appropriate balance between thermal insulation and thermal storage capacity.

17. Plan for climatically appropriate surface and air temperature.

18. Use appropriate thermal radiation strategies for heating buildings including passive solar design concepts wherever viable.

19. Provide adequate acoustical protection from harmful noise and vibration.

20. Utilize physiological and ergonomic knowledge in interior and furniture design.

21. Consider proportion, harmonic measure, order and shape in design.

## Environmental Protection, Social Responsibility and Energy Efficiency

22. Materials and methods of construction shall promote human health and well-being from the extraction of raw materials, through to end-of-building's life.

23. Avoid the use of building materials that deplete irreplaceable natural resources or are being harvested in an unsustainable manner.

24. Minimize energy consumption throughout the life of the building utilizing climate-based and energy efficient design, energy and water saving technologies and safe systems for renewable energy.

25. Consider the embodied energy and environmental life cycle costs when choosing all materials used in construction.

This recipe could be used for a new dwelling or a strategy to develop multi-generational communities. The old saying "it takes a village to raise a child" may be true but I believe "it takes a community of well-intentioned individuals to be sustainable for life."

That said, you will find beneficial information on wellintent.net should you need the services of a trained environmental health professional and more information on testing with meters for high levels of EMR/RF and who to contact regarding mould, designing homes and how to identify safe locations. [134]

## Do harmonizers work?

George and I discussed the problem with harmonizers, pendants, and gadgets sold as protection devices to reduce health effects or harmonize RFR in the local area. George said something I think everyone should know. If there was a product that protected people and the Profits @ Any Cost knew it worked, they'd buy it, or stop them from being sold. Their aim is to track you and control you. If it blocked signals, they'd lose control. Think this through - if transmissions could be blocked by a simple product, they'd lose money and control of the masses.

I have purchased many, and they do absolutely nothing. If they worked, I'd be selling them. If they worked, your phone wouldn't. If they worked canaries wouldn't need to persist. If you have purchased something and your phone still works, it's not doing anything, except making someone rich. If you still don't believe me, read Keith Cutter's Substack post. He goes into great detail. [135]

ORSAA, (Oceania Radiofrequency Scientific Advisory Association) also provide an excellent disclaimer about radiation protection products. [136]

> "ORSAA does not recommend or endorse any of these products of radiation 'protection'. Instead, we advocate for increased awareness of wireless technology and recommend

practices for safer use, such as keeping devices away from the body and limiting unnecessary exposure."

The military have ways and means of blocking frequencies, but according to George they produce high levels of radiation. Blocking or scrambling of signals is a tactic used in the military and the devices are not in the hands of normal people. Capabilities of energy weapons is way above my level of knowledge; therefore, I will not go deep into details. However, energy weapons and the development of them, has increased exponentially since WWII. Communications on the militaryaerospace.com website provide an insight into the capabilities of infrared shortwave (SWIR) technology. Infrared is also a radiofrequency on the radiofrequency spectrum. From the Military + Aerospace Electronics website; [137]

> "The development of laser-guided munitions was the first step in reducing collateral damage and improving weapon precision. In World War II it could take 9,000 bombs to hit a large target the size of an aircraft shelter. In Vietnam it took 300 bombs. By the mid 1990's it took only one laser-guided munition."

Weapons of mass destruction have existed for a long time and the powers that be, have had the power to destroy anything they please with Direct Energy Weapon (DEW) technology, and microwave technology is smack bang in the middle of it. We are in the midst of a great war, one that has been going on silently for a long time and if my information sources are correct, we need to prepare for a turning of the tide, metaphorically. We will need our wits about us if we wish to survive, and we'll need as many people as we can muster, at the highest level of learning, of unconscious competence, to help those not aware and not prepared, to create a sustainable future.

## PEOPLE IN THE KNOW – WARNING THE WORLD

During my investigations into crimes against humanity I became aware of the International Tribunal for Natural Justice (ITNJ), established in 2015, by a group of knowledgeable people aware of worldwide horrific injustices. The tribunal headed by Sacha Stone, Founder and Trustee of the ITNJ, and Justices: Sir John Walsh of Brannagh, a human rights advocate, and constitutional lawyer of international standing and Dr. Chris Cleverly, a barrister and leading advocate for human-rights, social justice and law reform, stands as a pivotal point in history, where good people commit to truth and integrity against a world of seemingly insurmountable corruption. I share because I care. If it were not for people sharing this information with me, I would be none the wiser. **Wiser is better.**

## ITNJ HEARINGS:

April 2018 the ITNJ Commission launched a Judicial Commission of Inquiry into Human Trafficking and Child Sex Abuse at an inaugural seating at Westminster, London. Filmed testimonies are available online at the ITNJ website: [138]

2019 ITNJ Judicial Commission of Inquiry into Weaponisation of the Biosphere (5G) video testimonies are available online at: [139]

June 2020 Emergency hearings were held into the Corona Pandemic and the planetary shutdown. Testimonies from expert witnesses worldwide provide a completely different picture than the one portrayed by governments and authorities worldwide. I highly recommend listening to the testimonies of people, either directly affected or experts in their field, that have not been able to speak publicly due to censorship by the mainstream media.

## WHAT EVERYONE NEEDS TO KNOW ABOUT COVID 19 AND 5G

In 2020 I was lucky enough to have friends who knew more than me about the COVID-19 plan. If you didn't have contacts in the know, all you knew about COVID-19 would have come from the mainstream media. As you've learned, mainstream media is controlled by the Deep State, also known as the Illuminati. Friends suggested I research Agenda 201, which actually stands for Agenda 21, and the 0 stands for the world. When I looked into Agenda 201, I discovered there was an Event 201, hosted by John Hopkins University. [140] This is what you will find if you go to the Event 201 website:

> The Johns Hopkins Center for Health Security in partnership with the World Economic Forum and the Bill and Melinda Gates Foundation hosted Event 201, a high-level pandemic exercise on October 18, 2019, in New York, NY. The exercise illustrated areas where public/private partnerships will be necessary during the response to a severe pandemic in order to diminish large-scale economic and societal consequences.

> In recent years, the world has seen a growing number of epidemic events, amounting to approximately 200 events annually. These events are increasing, and they are disruptive to health, economies, and society. Managing these events already strains global capacity, even absent a pandemic threat. Experts agree that it is only a matter of time before one of these epidemics becomes global—a pandemic with potentially catastrophic consequences. A severe pandemic; a planned operation, "Event 201," would require reliable cooperation among several industries, national governments, and key international institutions.

It's mind boggling to learn how they prepared in advance to fool the world into believing a coronavirus would get out of control, killing billions of people. Of course, billions didn't die, not because of social distancing or wearing a mask, but because it was a lie. Event 201 details how they planned to co-ordinate the worldwide event. What they were preparing for was a rollout of vaccines, supposedly to protect people from this nasty virus in the future. PROBLEM – REACTION – SOLUTION in action. Another load of baloney. It was a book by Dr Thomas Cowan and Sally Fallon Morell, *The Contagion Myth; Why Viruses (including "Coronavirus") Are Not the Cause of Disease,* [141] that cemented my belief that the real virus was 5G and a depopulation agenda. I believe Tom and Sally are on the money:

**Thomas S. Cowan, MD, and Sally Fallon Morell ask the question: are there really such things as "viruses"? Or are electro smog, toxic living conditions, and 5G actually to blame for COVID-19?**

My thoughts exactly; echoed by many around the world. Investigators like me didn't swallow the fabricated agenda. This was not the only source of truthful disclosure I followed, I was an avid listener to Sayer Ji, (pronounced Gee). Sayer's platform GreenMedInfo, was a source of good news regarding health, nutrition, natural immunity and famous for exposing the fake agendas by the medical system. [142] It was eventually shut down by the DS. Sayer tells his story on Substack to the Erased team. [143] Well worth listening to, because you will understand the atrocities of the DS and understand how they tried to silence those in the world that were exposing the truth. Sayer was listed as one of the Disinformation Dozen, exposing the truth about COVID-19 and the mNRA vaccine. The Disinformation Dozen are Conspiracy Realists, and they include: Rushid Buttar, Christiane Northrup, Robert F. Kennedy, Jr., Sherrie Tenpenny, Sayer Ji, Ty and Charlene Bollinger, Kelly Brogan, Joseph Mercola, Ben Tapper, Kevin Jenkins, Erin Elzabeth, and Rizza Islam. Meet this team of inspirational leaders, by reading an article by James Corbett on The Truth About Cancer website: [144]

James Corbett, famous for The Corbett Report, (an inside view of world events), alerted me to the dirty deeds of Bill Gates, and the Bill Gates Foundation. James is very much aware that we are in a global war, one that is perpetrated by governments on the people. [145]

## Who in the world do you need to listen to

If you think I am wrong about the enormity of the problem, why would there be hundreds of good people and pro-active organisations around the world shining a light on the dangers of EMF and 5G technology. Here is a short list taken from my database:

5G Space Appeal - Arthur Firstenberg: https://www.5gspaceappeal.org/the-appeal

Americans for Responsible Technology:

https://www.americansforresponsibletech.org/treasurechest

Broadband International Legal Action Network (BBILAN): https://www.bbilan.org/

EMFacts.com Consultancy Australia: https://www.emfacts.com/blog/

EMF Portal (Germany): https://www.emf-portal.org/en

Oceania Radiofrequency Scientific Advisory Association: https://www.orsaa.org/

Physicians' Health Initiative for Radiation and Environment: https://phiremedical.org/

Radiation Refuge: https://www.radiationrefuge.com/myrrhee-victoria-refuge

Safe Tech International; Recording history as it happens:

https://safetechinternational.org/global-protest-days-against-5g-a-history/

WEEP initiative Canada: http://www.weepinitiative.org/index.html

We Say No To 5G In Australia: https://www.wesaynoto5ginaustralia.com/

Safe Living Technologies: https://safelivingtechnologies.com/

https://empvictims.org/ is the most recent website I added to my database, and it's one of the most important ones, because it highlights the plight of EHS people, mostly in Europe, however not all people declaring EHS is a humanitarian crisis live in Europe. In May 2025 there are over

4,000 signatures, I'm one of them, so is Keith Cutter, who sent me a link to sign the appeal, that recognises we have a humanitarian crisis regarding effects from RF EMR exposure. Keith recorded a video, as have many others, of their life as an electromagnetic pollution refugee. All EHS stories reveal life-threatening situations, and injustices in the way EHS people are treated. This is not a new phenomenon, it's been happening for decades.

*Never doubt that a small group of thoughtful,*
*committed people can change the world.*
*Indeed, it is the only thing that ever has.*
~ Margaret Mead

My list of videos, websites, testimonies and scientific research is huge, the above is just a snippet. One site I came across listed over 42,000 studies which is amazing but sadly nothing has stopped the onslaught and release of more wireless technology, at least not in Australia, UK, Europe, Canada and USA. There is a quiet rebellion worldwide, of activists, scientists and some experts providing sanctuary, by creating White Zones or EMF Refuges in Europe and Costa Rica, one is a Quiet Zone of 13,000-square-miles around the Green Bank Observatory in West Virginia, USA. [146] Here you'll find Mountain Quest Retreat, a 450-acre farm without Wi-Fi and smart devices and no mobile phone connection. Realistically one or two quiet zones doesn't solve the problem for canaries worldwide, seeking a safe place to live.

Australian Bruce Evans, became sensitive in 2007 and attempted to create a sanctuary in Myrrhee, Victoria but the location was within range of a telephone transmission tower high on a hill overlooking the property and not suitable for people with EHS. Because Bruce cannot live in an EMF polluted environment, he built a faraday cage on his property to survive. His website provides a platform for people to post all sorts of information, from ES publications to profiles of people worldwide, some wanting housing, some with stories and some who offer services. [147]

## The science and ethics we need

If you're like me, and have been attempting to live the best life possible, I have some juicy information that may help you take a step on the road to living healthier for longer. Reading *In Love with Betty the Crow by ABC science reporter, Robyn Williams,*[148] I came across some fantastic discoveries. Betty by the way, was a Caledonian crow used in an experiment with other crows to retrieve meat from a plastic tube. During an experiment male crows took the wires with hooks with them and left only strait pieces of wire. Betty being the smart bird that she was, took the straight wire and bent it to create a hook and retrieved the meat. That's a metaphor for *Smart birds find alternatives.* In Robyn's book I learned about Elizabeth Blackburn's ground breaking discovery of telomeres and telomerase, crucial for preventing cellular aging. Elizabeth was born in Tasmania, went to school in Launceston, studied in Melbourne, in the field of biochemistry, before receiving her PhD from Darwin College at the University of Cambridge. Elizabeth reached great heights during her professional career, and served as Professor Emeritus at the University of California, San Franscisco in 2015. She was awarded the 2009 Nobel Prize in Physiology or Medicine, sharing it with Carol W. Freider and Jack W. Szostak. Elizabeth was instrumental in discovering telomerase, through studying the telomere, a structure at the end of chromosomes that protects the chromosome; a chromosome is a thread-like structure made up of proteins and DNA that carries genetic information from one cell generation to the next. Specifically stem cells are the foundation cells for every cell, tissue and organ in the body. Stem cells are intelligent cells able to be programmed, therefore hugely important for cell regeneration. Imagine a caplet on the end of a shoelace that protects the shoelace and stops if from fraying. Similarly, telomerase works by adding base pairs to the overhand of DNA, slowing ageing. You can read more about Elizabeth and Telomerase on her website or Wikipedia, but what's important about her discovery is, she detected how to get more life out of life. From Wikipedia: [149]

Blackburn comments on ageing reversal and care for one's telomeres through lifestyle: managing chronic stress, exercising, eating better and getting enough sleep. While studying telomeres and the replenishing enzyme, telomerase, Blackburn discovered a vital role played by these protective caps that revolved around one central idea: ageing of cells...Elizabeth co-authored, The Telomere Effect: A Revolutionary Approach to Living Younger, Healthier, Longer, with health psychologist Dr. Elissa S. Epel... The book hones in on many of the effects that poor health can have on telomeres and telomerase activity. Since telomeres shorten with every division of a cell, replenishing these caps is essential to long term cell growth.

Through research and data, Blackburn explained that people that lead stressful lives exhibit less telomerase functioning in the body, which leads to a decrease in the dividing capabilities of the cell. Once telomeres shorten drastically, the cells can no longer divide, meaning the tissues they replenish with every division would therefore die out, highlighting the ageing mechanism in humans. To increase telomerase activity in people with stress-filled lives, Blackburn suggests moderate exercise, even 15 minutes a day, which has been proven to stimulate telomerase activity and replenish the telomere.

Blackburn states that unhappiness in lives also has an effect on the shortening of telomeres. In a study done on divorced couples, their telomere length was "significantly shorter" compared to couples in healthy relationships, and Blackburn states, "There's an obvious stressor ... we are intensely social beings." She suggests positivity in daily life increases health. While increasing the amount of exercise, decreasing stress, and tobacco use, and maintaining a balanced sleep schedule, Blackburn explains that telomere length can be maintained, leading to a decrease in cell aging. Blackburn also tells readers to be wary of clinical pills that proclaim to lengthen telomeres and protect the body from aging. She says that these pills and creams have no scientific proof of being anti-aging supplements and that the key to preserving our telomeres and stimulating telomerase activity comes from leading a healthy life.

I love a good ending. What I discovered from going to Ikaria, reading *In Love with Betty the Crow* and learning about Elizbeth Blackburn's research is: **Laughter is good medicine**. Loving what you do, is good medicine. Being in good company is good medicine. Setting your own rules is liberating. Goodness matters, and it's catching among good people. I believe Elizabeth Blackburn is a smart bird, and we can all benefit from her discoveries.

In Elizabeth's article on Wikipedia, George W. Bush sacked Elizabeth from her position on the President's Council on Bioethics because of her disapproval of the Bush administration's position against stem cell research. This prompted outrage over her removal by many scientists. Elizabeth was on the money about scientific research:

> From her bio, Blackburn noted: "There is a growing sense that scientific research—which, after all, is defined by the quest for truth—is being manipulated for political ends" … "There is evidence that such manipulation is being achieved through the stacking of the membership of advisory bodies and through the delay and misrepresentation of their reports."

Elizabeth was smart enough to not trust George W. Bush. Betty the crow outsmarted the male birds to get the meat. People in Ikaria made their own rules, and didn't rely on government assistance which helped them live longer than most. We need to outsmart those that designed millimetre wave technology, and use our God given natural intelligence, common sense and love for humanity to rise above conformity, reducing the power the Deep State has over us.

In summary, changing the paradigm of profit, means we need to change what profit means to us. Profit in the dictionary, means to gain an advantage, not just gain money. If we are to gain an advantage, we must question everything we have been taught by the monopoly of power and begin an unlearning process to relearn what is good for us. People in the know, exposed what has been going on under the veil of deception. Once you know how corrupt the DS is, how they use media, medicine and mind manipulation to control your thinking, all you need to do is change your thinking and they lose control. Stop believing the medical industry is a health industry. Stop believing you can't live without your mobile phone in your pocket. Stop believing the government cares. **Start** believing in your God given natural intelligence, and start taking control of the results you get. Gaining from an alternative education is looking like a very good way to turn things around. Maybe not overnight but with help from honest to goodness people exposing the culture and corruption dished out by the Deep State, we may all develop unconscious competence over time.

Imagine if we unite and work as one, like Vandana Shiva suggested in Oneness vs the 1%; the world may one day be a wonderful, healthy and loving place to live. David Sorensen, creator of Stop World Control website,[150] had a dream that one day our world would be a glorious place to live, where humans live in harmony with nature and there's peace on Earth. I'm focused on helping create that reality. Watch the documentaries on StopWorldControl.com to elevate your consciousness. I guarantee it's an education you don't want to miss.

# CONCLUSION

Canaries, (I like to think of them as smart birds), are a sign something is drastically wrong in the world. The history of health effects from EMF goes back a long way and organisations we are meant to trust, take no notice of the enormous volume of science exposing the truth. Fact is, governments fail us, over and over again. Chapter two presented overwhelming evidence of crimes against humanity. You learned how man-made frequencies affect our biology and what the repercussions are. You gained some insights into how they pulled the wool over our eyes and who the villains are. Chapter three was designed to make you smarter than your smart phone. First by exposing 7 Threats to a Good Life and to learn what George and I have done to tame the invisible wireless beast. Have I provided enough evidence to change your thinking about the way you use technology? I hope so. Maybe! You've gained an awareness that we are supernatural beings, much more intelligent than we've been led to believe, and more intelligent than any drug, GP or politician.

The Age of Aquarius is upon us, which means we are not alone in this massive awakening of humanity. You are now prepped to aid in the wake-up and to lend a hand by uniting and thinking in harmony with nature, canaries, and the stars. It feels good to be aware and awake but we still have a few hurdles to overcome.

People learn in different ways and for different reasons, some love to learn more, some seem to dig their heals in, resisting anything that looks like an education. Some want to know what's the advantage of learning a specific subject, in other words, *"what's in it for me"* while some need to realise what the repercussions are for them, should they do nothing. Learning happens in stages and I'm aware many people would already have an understanding that things are not as they should be in the world, but have no idea in what direction to go. That's why signposts are handy. I found a big one, and added it to my final words, but have you realised each chapter was a signpost taking you on a journey of enlightenment, - one that many people never make, because they had no idea the truth has been covered up.

Without the signposts in chapter 4 to master your mind, you would still be unaware of how we've been conditioned to not question anything. It's a small example of the mechanisms of control they've used to mislead us. Blind spots, biases and cognitive dissonance highlight how our thinking can work against us, and why a controlled education can hinder gaining a real education. Robert Cialdini introduced us to a concept of pluralistic ignorance – in short – a perception, that if everyone else is doing it, it must be ok to ignore crimes outside our window, believing it's not my problem. Or it's not my problem, I'm ok (attitude). Additionally, Skinner and others influenced operant conditioning, learned helplessness and a belief in doing the same thing over and over, even if it's not working in our favour. Now you know irregular rewarded behaviour is the hardest of all to eradicate, it's possible you could slowly unhitch from the reward systems that keep you sucked inside the vortex of lies, deceit, and manipulation of the sickness system, identify the propaganda agenda (aka the nightly news misinformation machine) and become supernatural. It won't happen overnight, I'm an example of that, but it can happen. Changing the paradigm of Profits @ Any Cost could be as simple as changing what you believe to be true. Or simply gaining an alternative education, to gain a distinct advantage.

My suggestion at this stage in the Great Awakening is to take control of your mental and physical development. Create an environment sustainable for life to dodge as many threats to life as you can. Use technology wisely – and adopt a less is best mentality. Betty the Crow was a sign post; she used intelligence to beat the big boys, metaphorically speaking. Self-regulate like people in Ikaria, and choose to do what you love, and laugh more, seek good company, and don't tolerate the George W. Bushes of the world.

If not for canaries, telling their stories and enlightening the masses, we could all be headed for a hypothetical cliff. Why do I say cliff? On my journey of discovery, I learned the art of slaughter from the North American Indians who survived by killing buffalo, also known as bison, by herding them over a cliff. They are large beasts and not easy to capture. The Indians studied their habits, how they grazed in herds with their heads close to the ground and how they followed the leader when in danger. When they were spooked the Indians would steer them toward a cliff. Buffalo out in front would not see the cliff until it was too late, and the force of the herd behind would push them over the edge. Herd mentality can, in many instances, be a recipe for disaster.

Most people are headed for the proverbial cliff, with eyes firmly fixated on the screens in their hands, they have no idea the cliff exists or that marketing and persuasion is literally herding them in the wrong direction. Profits @ Any Cost know exactly what they are doing, and it's working, which is truly scary.

At some point in the future many will recognise they trusted the wrong people, because they never questioned the narrative or the people in power.

# FINAL WORDS

*The Perpetual Wheel of Fortune Designed by the Elites*

Little by little, those with the most money have controlled the world. This graphic shows you how they do it with our hard-earned money, sweat and fears.

AI-technology may sound inviting and seem like it's the next best thing to make us brighter and less stressed. I think not. During my planning to write this book, I engaged a coach and after the first draft, paid for a manuscript assessment. Both provided insights to improve my writing skills, and alerted me to what needed to be shared; however, I was not expecting to be rewarded by learning even more about our planned demise. I'm alluding to how unconscious competence in the area of problem-reaction-solution awareness works. I put two and two together and came up with big costs and big problems for humanity regarding AI programs. This happened when my manuscript assessor mentioned a Microsoft study in 2015, showing an astounding decline in the attention span of people down to an average of 8.25 seconds, I knew it was not an accident. Even goldfish have a 9 second attention span. We're headed in the wrong direction, and it doesn't take an Einstein to figure out that it's a calculated move, just like the expected rise in dementia and pharmaceuticals needed to help people manage emotionally, as documented in Dr Pri Bandara's forward for this book. The pharmaceutical industry is planning for an increase in the need for **psychotropic medicines.** Go back and read the forward again, this time with open eyes and you will see what I'm alluding to. Why would they be preparing doctors and researchers for this need, if it wasn't planned? How could they know this in advance if it wasn't a created problem? Hint, wireless microwave frequencies are harmful to the brain. It's the Problem the DS have created. Then comes the Reaction i.e. people can't cope. Learning ability in young adults decreases, and workplaces need help with AI that's been developed to help them out, to control what they write and what they believe, i.e. the Solution. We have a problem in the making. More people will be diagnosed with autoimmune disorders (suggested by Dr Miller), caused by RFR. The Reaction: more research will need to be conducted to solve the problem, and more drugs and visits to the doctor will be the Solution. This is the wheel of fortune continually evolving to feed the pockets of Profits @ Any Cost.

Ironically there's a good side to technology. I remember the days before the internet, emails, mobile phones and social media and I don't believe going backwards would help. It would be like going back to the horse and cart and snail mail. Technology brought us into the Information Age, and instant access to each other. That is not a bad thing. What needs to happen, as has happened in the past, we need to assess what is good and what is bad. As long as we use technology wisely, protect people and children from Wi-Fi, smart screens, cyber bullies and brainwashing tactics, we may be able to nudge them in the right direction, away from addictions, the dark agenda, and control by mainstream media and AI. If we teach each and every person how wonderfully powerful nature and human biology is, and how much potential we have if technology is used wisely, we will survive. We may even find we have psychic skills and mind power capabilities beyond comprehension.

What if the introduction of 5G warfare was designed to shut down the mass awakening and completely eliminate our God given intelligence and intuition. AI is artificial intelligence; even the name tells us it's a stupid step in the wrong direction. Maybe they knew they were losing control of the narrative and had no option but to attempt to create another war and another pandemic as they have done in the past, to take attention away from the truth and injustices worldwide. AI is not designed to make you a better person, it's another control mechanism and deliberately used to delete your innate intelligence and talent. There may be some valid uses for AI-technology that pass the SNIFF test. This means it would have be Sustainable, Nurturing, Intuitive and Family Friendly, and as long as we all agree it meets Murphy's policies - AI in some instances might be ok.

Murphy's policies came about because I realised a long time ago, my original business training and policies used in business development would not meet today's needs. Murphy is my grandson, and was nineteen months old at the time. These policies were created to ensure his future potential was not jeopardised by Profits @ Any Cost.

Murphy's policies remove Profits @ Any Cost mentality, and place our children as the benchmark. Measurable policies are needed to govern the hierarchy of control in business to initiate policies that benefit everyone, especially our children and those that care for them.

## MURPHY'S POLICIES

### Murphy's No. 1 Policy

All our policies are governed by moral and ethical decisions that protect life and prevent harm to people and planet, for generations to come. This is a *protection and prevention at any cost*, policy.

### Murphy's Quality Policy

If it's not good for Murphy and his mates, we don't use it, support it or promote it. End of Policy.

### Murphy's Health Policy

We do all we can to live in harmony with Nature. We do not give death and disease any assistance. End of Policy.

### Murphy's Money Policy

We do not give money to others that will disrupt the Health Policy. End of Policy.

### Murphy's Asset Protection Policy

Our greatest assets are:

- Our children
- Our health
- Our collective brainpower
- Our planet

Our Asset Protection Policy must ensure all our assets are biologically, environmentally, financially, ethically and morally secure. End of policy.

### Murphy's Safety Policy

Safety is everyone's responsibility in every situation and every location.

Currently safety in the home is not controlled by a Workplace Health and Safety Plan and there's nothing in the WH&S Act or Regulations to keep parents, grandparents and our children safe.

This needs to change. Safety Management Systems need upgrading to meet biological sustainability as a priority.

Ensuring our environment and our future is safe requires an attitude and a culture based on prevention being the best medicine. You cannot focus on safety without a focus on Risk Management. End of policy.

**Murphy's Risk Management Policy**

We cannot risk authorities ruling our future; we cannot risk a Profits @ Any Cost dictatorship; we cannot risk waiting for governments, or world health authorities to change the laws to protect Murphy and his mates. That's why we have appointed Mother Nature as our Risk Management Advisor and the science of Building Biology and natural selection as our benchmark for home creation. It's the only way the world will be safe. End of Policy

**Murphy's Future Policy**

The future is ours to create. We can only do that if we knowingly and willingly influence evolution positively. It's simple; do today what pays off tomorrow.

This Policy must benefit our children and our children's children and future generations. We are only here for a short period of time; make that time influence seven generations into the future.

**Murphy's Sustainability Policy**

Sustainability is a life-long game requiring an evolutionary mind-set. Sustainability matters because being unsustainable is not very satisfying at the least, and deadly at worst. Something that is unsustainable cannot continue at the same rate without diabolical consequences. Four critical focus areas for human sustainability include:

- **Sustainable health** of our biological systems and our children's reproduction potential. If we fail to look after our children, and our planet, we are failing to look after the future of humanity.

- **Sustainable development** to reduce our environmental footprint and limit biological effects on all living things. The opposite is unsustainable development, when progress is at the expense of future generations. For example, damage to the environment and ecosystems due to pollution, including EMR pollution and irresponsible planning and environmental degradation could be the worst inheritance our children are saddled with.

- **Sustainable education system** to develop sustainable children, sustainable parents, sustainable thinking resulting in sustainable communities.

- **Sustainable economic systems** to ensure we don't leave our children a debt they cannot pay off; the opposite is the desire to win or profit at any cost, and that cost could be the loss of our children's future and their future potential. Healthy children = a healthy future.

In a nutshell, our children should not have to fix man-made stuff-ups. If we do not value the natural environment and the planet that supports us, life will become unliveable. This is why developing strategies and systems to enhance health, support sustainable development and re-imagine economic viability is a win win for humanity and planet Earth. This is not the End of Murphy's policies; this is the beginning of the future we could ideally create.

**At this stage in our awakening, there is a need to create order out of chaos:**

What if more people cared and shared canary stories, in lunchrooms, on worksites, in schools, sporting clubs, health care and child care centres. Cartoons throughout the book have been created for people to share. Place them on noticeboards or on social media to help light the fire of learning. All content is available on wellintent.net to use and share. You can make your own memes, funny photos or blogs to help raise awareness.

What if more people knew microwave RFR was responsible for existing health conditions. Sharing this information will help those that are totally blind to the brainwashing tactics by the hierarchy of control. Knowing the truth is rather inconvenient, but trust me, knowing is way better than suffering from ignorance.

What if everyone reading this book switched to safe use of technology and taught others to do the same.

What if more people collaborated to create sustainable communities.

What if more people learned the art and science of Building Biology, to help detect the invisible beast and help others create naturally healthy environments.

What if more people created safe EMF environments to help people with EHS, go to work, shop in local areas without Wi-Fi, and attend social events or have a holiday in a safe low EMF holiday home or resort.

Creating safe holiday rentals may help people determine if EMF or mould is the cause of ill-health. Ironically Keith Cutter from EMF Remedy had that exact same thought. The Universe seems to be hatching a plan. Read more about Keith's idea on Substack: [151] [152]

https://keithcutter.substack.com/p/emf-challenge-facilities-a-vision

What if more people decided to create a better world by using Murphy's policies in businesses, schools, childcare centres, and family homes. Or used Murphy's policies, substituting their own children or grandchildren's names to write new life-enhancing methodologies.

What if more people initiate the introduction of safe EMF/RFR into Workplace Health & Safety Systems. Work Safe legislation worldwide is unanimous; workers have a right to a safe workplace, and risk management and risk reduction is a high priority.

What if we trained more architects, designers and builders to create safer, healthier, biologically sustainable homes and buildings.

What if we the people trained conscientious, open-minded doctors to identify environmental toxins, encouraging them to refer patients to Building Biologists, EMF Technicians and Mould Testing experts to find the cause of ill-health.

Dr. William Rea, (1935-2018) founder of the Center for Environmental Health, in Dallas, Texas, addressed the North American Building Biology Conference in 2011: Dr. Rae spoke on environmental pollutants, causing neurodegenerative diseases; Alzheimer's and Parkinson's disease, and explained how exposure to EMF causes dead nerves in the brain. Dr. Rae created the term Barrel Effect, meaning when the barrel is full it can't take any more. The barrel is our body, and when our body is filled to the brim with environmental pollutants, the immune system fails. The result is disease, and if nothing changes, and the toxic load is not reduced, death is the outcome. Once upon a time it was pesticides, gas (petrol) fumes, formaldehyde and mould, but these days it's EMF. Once your body is full (overloaded), disease manifests. He suggests mould is the most potent microbial toxin on Earth because moulds disintegrate everything (alive or dead). Microbial toxins directly damage a host's tissue, disabling the immune system. When asked by a conference attendee, *"is the increase in asthma, allergies, and autism spectrum disorder directly related to EMF,"* he said, without hesitation, *"yes."* [153] *(Building Biology Conference)*

Dr. William Rae confirmed all of my suspicions (even more than I've listed above) that governments, and the medical and pharmaceutical industry do all they can to keep us from knowing the truth about environmental poisons and health effects from electro-pollution. The USA government defunded the EPA when they started to investigate the effects of EMF. This is a signpost, we're on the right track. You can watch the conference on YouTube. Thanks must go to the Building Biology Institute in North America for sharing.

More people are recognising the need for Building Biologists to work alongside doctors to solve environmental health issues. The message below, posted on the Building Biology Institute website (USA) makes it pretty clear, doctors can't solve health problems alone.

"Our institute and more than twenty of our professionally certified alumni were heralded time and again by speakers at last year's three-day EMF Conference, in Santa Cruz, California. Dr. Devra Davis (EH Trust) captured it best when she asked our Building Biologists to stand up, and told the more than 300 assembled MDs and other healthcare and EMF professionals, 'I want to thank the Building Biologists for being here. And I want to say this: The new model for integrative medicine is going to have to be Building Biologists hand-in-hand [with health providers].' And Dr. Davis went further to encourage her audience to meet and partner with our alumni."

Many things would change if responsibility for the results we get was not handed over to others, especially those that have no idea what they don't know.

At this point in time, we have two choices:

1. Accept responsibility for creating a better future, or

2. Do nothing and suffer the consequences.

**Accepting responsibility is as simple as:**

1. Upskilling to learn the basics of environmental health. Including how to test, to detect harmful RF and EMF and identify safe non-toxic products. Or identify if mould is the cause of health problems.

2. Learn how to identify if your home or your workplace, or both, is in a safe location or in a danger zone and too close to telephone transmission towers or high voltage transmission lines, known to cause leukemia and cancer.

3. Turn your business into a safe, non-toxic environment. Making it a more harmonious and nurturing workplace. Healthy workers are good for business.

4. What if more people learned how to build a business that stood out from the rest. Instead of following the age-old narrative that time is money. Time is not money, time is life. More life gives you more time. Ask anyone battling cancer. What do they want? More time with loved ones or more time to fulfill their dreams. Creating a business that gives people more life could be life-changing on a grand scale.

5.  What if more parents taught their children how to use commonsense and critical thinking skills, and how and why they need to question everything.

Much more could be achieved if we change our beliefs about health and well-being and who really has our best interests at heart. Question everything before accepting anything as a fact. Learn the art of critical thinking before giving away your power to the systems that fail us. Value kindness and gratitude as the greatest gifts, instead of valuing profits at any cost. Elevate natural and higher intelligence to be the most important intelligence of all. If we educate young adults to be responsible from an early age, we have the potential to make the world a better place. The world we create going forward will be the world children inherit in the future.

IMAGINE if we had an army of good people, doing today what pays off tomorrow, to create a world free of Profits @ Any Cost mentality. A world where peace and harmony reign supreme, where children, and health are the highest priorities. Where Environmental Health Centres and Holistic Health and Natural Healing Clinics are supported and funded by good governments. A world where Healthy Building Education is normal and Healthy Building Centres supply non-toxic products and dangerous chemicals are outlawed. Only when we take a step in the right direction will right things happen.

## Becoming Chery Lanne

Between 2012 and 2014, I discovered a way of thinking I had never experienced before. An alternate education changed my beliefs and my perspective on life. I became a different person. I no longer wanted to be Cheryl Anne, I wanted a new name to live a new life, unhindered by my past. My dilemma, I was a director of three companies, manager and partner of a self-managed superannuation fund and trustee of a family trust. Changing my name was complicated.

It's amazing how the Universe delivers a solution when you need it, especially if you're open to receiving it. I met Josephine, a giver of True

Light, also referred to as Mahikari. Mahikari comes from Japan and literally means "True Light": "Ma" (True) – "Hikari" (Light). Mahikari refers to the Light of God, the Creator of all existence. This Light has been referred to in all kinds of religious teachings through the ages. God's Light is the spiritual energy or vibration of God's wisdom, love and will. It exists throughout the universe and is the fundamental power that creates and sustains life. Life force energy, also known as zero-point energy is in us and around us. We are not separate from this energy, just as we are not separate from nature.

Josphine suggested it is not a religion but a practice. When I was given True Light by Josephine, I didn't feel anything and asked what it would do for me and she said, *"whatever you want it to do."* I had no idea what that meant, but that night, in the middle of the night, I woke with the idea of changing my name from Cheryl Anne to Chery Lanne. I simply moved the little l on Cheryl to Anne, and changed it to a capital L to create Chery Lanne. This is the power of receiving True Light, wisdom from the universe delivered to your inbox. Being aware of this magical energy changes everything.

Additionally, it was Gregg Braden, a renowned author, researcher of ancient text and educator, that I learned; God Eternal – Within the Body. A discovery translation from ancient scripts. These discoveries explained why words are important, example; telling yourself *"I can"* instead of *"I can't."* Asking for what you want; talking about the future you wish to create, positively, not negatively. Masaru Emoto confirmed this concept with his frozen water crystals. In The Hidden Messages in Water, Emoto wrote; *"we have the capacity to change the world with Love and Gratitude… words are vibrations that change water into beautiful crystals."* When you learn how magical (God like) you are, and how powerful nature is energetically, you have the recipe to heal, and to create a new future or live a great life.

Nikola Tesla said *"if you want to find the secrets of the universe, think in terms of energy, frequency and vibration."* Two books by Eileen Day McKusick bring this statement to life and into cognitive comprehension. McKusick's first book, TUNING THE HUMAN BIOFIELD; *Healing with Vibrational*

*Sound Therapy* and her second book, ELECTRIC BODY, ELECTRIC HEALTH; *Using the Electromagnetism Within (and Around) You to Rewire, Recharge, and Raise Your Voltage,* provide insights into sound therapy, and our connection with the *unified field* also known as *the field* that composes the things we see and the space between them. McKusick's research provides the evidence that all is connected to energy, frequency and vibration. We are Light Beings, light carries information. McKusick states *"Energy follows thought. What we put our focus on grows. What we neglect declines."* **Here we have the solution we've been looking for.**

Understanding energy, explains the power of hands-on healing, how Feng Shui, (pronounced Fung Shway) an ancient Chinese practice of harmonising an environment, improves the flow of qi; vital life force energy. Use the knowledge you've gained wisely and harness the laws of nature to create harmony and prosperity. Everyone can create it, if they believe they can. What you tell yourself (words) you become. This explains how the placebo effect works or unintentionally how the nocebo effect impacts biology and why man-made EMF depletes the flow of vital life force energy, and why natural Earth energy heals.

You have the power within you to become a different person. It's the power of being human, and it is what Profits @ Any Cost try to destroy. Once you know how natural intelligence works, how thoughts hold power, and how to decipher truth from lies, you have conscious competence to control and influence every move. This means you have ability to change outcomes, and wisdom no one can take away, unless you give them permission.

We have some work to do to right the wrongs in the world. Don't give up or give in. If we do that, who will protect the children. We all need to step up and become a voice for good. If you are still doubtful or still not sure who you can trust, I urge you to read Ty Bollinger's book; *Monumental Myths of the Modern Medical Mafia and Mainstream Media and the Multitude of Lying Liars That Manufactured Them.* [154] This book exposes more juicy truths than I have, and it's worth reading if you can handle what they don't want you to know.  I hope you use this information as a spark to light your fire for learning more.

Thank you for reading A CANARY INVESTIGATES, God bless, stay safe.
– Chery Lanne

Visit wellintent.net to find links to videos, websites, books and the scientific research listed in the Endnotes. Learn more about healthy buildings; how to test for high levels of EMF/EMR; how to get life back after it's been sucked out of you. If you're interested in becoming the super natural being you are designed to be, don't stop learning. Canaries need support and children need your protection. Please share far and wide.

It's not the end – it's time to practice; to gain unconscious competence. The solution to save humanity.

# ACKNOWLEDGMENTS

First and foremost, I wish to thank my partner of 46 years and love of my life. Without him, this book and my increased level of learning would not be possible. He is my business partner and building brains-trust, willing and able to implement my recommendations to build a safe place for me to live, for which I am extremely grateful.

Founders of the science of Building Biology are held in high esteem

Eben Pagan. Business Entrepreneur

Nicole Bijlsma, PhD. Founder of Australian College of Environmental Studies

Oceanic Radiofrequency Scientific Advisory Association (ORSAA)

Don Maisch, PhD. EMFacts.com ORSAA Executive Team

Priyanka (Pri) Bandara, PhD. ORSAA Executive Team

Robert O. Becker, Scientist, Teacher and Author

Magna Havas. PhD. Educator, Electrosensitivity Canada

Devra Davis, PhD. Environmental Health Trust

Olle Johansson; Professor of Basic and Applied Neuroscience from the Karolinska Institute, Royal Institute of Technology Stockholm, Sweden

Lloyd Burrell: electricsense.com

Nick Pineault: The EMF Guy

Outstanding authors, scientists and researchers worldwide; too long a list to mention.

My friends, colleagues and clients who taught me heaps along the way: Peggy and Pete, Bec and Blair (deceased), Michele, Janey, Bronwyn, Richard (deceased), Susen, Nicole, Paul, Jenny, Vicky, Sara and Karen. Sorry if I forgot anyone.

George Parker, Warrant Officer, Australian Army, EMF elder and Activist. (26th May 1937 - 1st August 2025). George was a true gentleman and a fighter for truth and justice. Will be sadly missed.

# GLOSSARY OF TERMS

2G, 3G, 4G, 5G: The G, stands for Generation and rollout of the $2^{nd}$, $3^{rd}$, $4^{th}$, $5^{th}$ stages of wireless technology. As the generations progressed wireless transmission became more secure, faster and more reliable. When $1^{st}$ Generation technology was offered it was an analogue service and it was the first wireless communication system. The only 1G cellular network is still operating is in Russia.

5G: $5^{th}$ Generation of wireless technology. As of the $25^{th}$ October 2019 the Australian Government declared that an increased level of band width will be made available for spectrum licencing to facilitate the rollout of 5G across Australia. 5G Rollout: Spectrum release by Australian Government. (25.1 to 27.5)

ACES: Australian College of Environmental Studies

ARPANSA: Australian Radiation Protection and Nuclear Safety Agency

CARCINOGEN: a substance or agent that can cause cells to become cancerous by altering their genetic structure therefore multiplying continuously and becoming malignant. Examples: asbestos, DDT and tobacco smoke (Dictionary). Carcinogens may increase the risk of cancer by directly damaging cells (DNA).

CIRS: Chronic Inflammatory Response Syndrome

DECT: Digital enhanced cordless telecommunications (e.g. cordless phone & base – both emit RFR)

ECG: Electrocardiogram; a test that measures the rate, rhythm, and electrical activity of the heart.

EEG: Electroencephalogram, brain activity test that measures electrical activity in the brain

EMF: Electromagnetic Field: An electromagnetic field is a physical field produced by electrically charged objects. It affects the behaviour of charged objects in the vicinity of the field.

EMR: Electromagnetic Radiation: is the radiant energy released by certain electromagnetic processes. Visible light is electromagnetic radiation, as is invisible light, such as radio waves, microwaves and X-rays.

EMRS: Electromagnetic Radiation Specialist

ES: Electrical Sensitivity / electro sensitivity

EHS: Electrical Hypersensitivity / electromagnetic hypersensitivity

FIXED WIRELESS: NBN uses fixed wireless systems utilising 4G/5G technology to transmit data over radio signals from a transmission tower to an NBN outdoor antenna fitted to premises by approved technicians. The signal from the antenna needs to be wired to an NBN connection box installed inside the premises, before being wired to other devices or data points. Never opt for wireless connections. They could be fatal. Fixed wireless is beam forming technology used from point-to-point signal transmissions through the air over a terrestrial microwave platform, rather than through copper or optical fibre. Beam forming microwaves are more biologically impactful, therefore transmitters need to be well above the ground to ensure people do not enter or pass through the microwaves.

GSM: Global System for Mobile Communications

IoT: Internet of Things is a system of interrelated computing devices, mechanical and digital machines, objects, animals or people that are provided with unique identifiers (UIDS) and the ability to transfer data over a network without requiring human-to-human or human-to-computer interaction. More simply IoT is a system designed to network interconnected things (including people) and devices which are embedded with sensors, software, network connectivity and necessary electronics that enables them to collect and exchange data making them responsive. It's about control using MIMO.

LTE: Long Term Evolution, LTE is a 4G wireless communications standard developed by the 3rd Generation Partnership Project (3GPP) that's designed to provide up to 10x the speed of 3G networks for mobile devices such as smartphones, tablets, laptop computers and wireless hot-spotting.

MCS: Multiple chemical Sensitivity

MIMO: Multiple Input Multiple Output. WiMAX technology makes use of MIMO by utilising the multiple signal paths that exist. MIMO enables operation with lower signal strength levels, and allows for higher data rates.

NBN: National Broadband Network

SBM 2015: Building Biology Evaluation Guidelines – Baubiologie IBM:

https://buildingbiology.com/building-biology-standard/

TETRA: Terrestrial Trunked Radio or Trans European Trunked Radia, is a global standard for digital trunked radio. It uses an advanced set of features such as secure voice and data transmission to manage the challenges of modern mobile radios.

UMTS: Universal Mobile Telecommunications Service is a third-generation (3G) broadband, packet-based transmission of text, digitized voice, video and multimedia at data rates up to megabits per second (Mbps).

URL: web address to a particular page or website

Wi-Fi: Wireless Fidelity, means you can access or connect to a network using radio waves, without using wires.

WiMAX: Worldwide Interoperability for Microwave Access, is a technology for point to multipoint wireless networking.

WLAN: Wireless Local Area Network. Wireless LAN is a network that allows devices to connect and communicate wirelessly. It is the opposite of a wired LAN which uses Ethernet cables. Devices on WLAN communicate via Wi-Fi.

WHO: World Health Organisation

## Abbreviations, Terminology and SI Units (International System of Units)

ELF Extra Low Frequency = electromagnetic radiation (radio waves) with frequencies from 3 to 300 Hz

Flux Density is the amount of magnetic, electric or other flux passing through a unit area.

Flux: (in physics) is the presence of a force field in a specified physical medium. Or the flow of energy through a surface. In electronics, the term applies to any electrostatic field and magnetic field. In short it is the action or process of flowing or flowing out (energy).

Frequency in Hertz:

1 Hertz (Hz) The number of sinusoidal cycles completed by electromagnetic waves in 1 second

1 kHz (kilohertz) = 1000 Hz,

1 MHz (megahertz) = 1,000,000 Hz

1 GHz (gigahertz) = 1,000,000,000 Hz

Magnetic flux density is the measurement of magnetic fields in units of nano Tesla (nT) or milligauss (mG).

Magnetic flux density is also measured in older units, the Gauss. Many measuring instruments are calibrated in milligauss ($1mG = 0.1\mu T = 100nT$).

Milligauss = mG (m = a thousandth) measurement of magnetic field e.g., 0.2 mG No Concern

Nano Tesla = nT (n = one billionth of a Tesla)

Tesla = the SI of magnetic flux density. 1 Tesla = 10000 gauss; Micro Tesla = µT (µ = a millionth)

20 nanotesla = 0.2 milligauss (safe for sleeping areas)

## Understanding the Radio Frequency Spectrum (compliments of George Parker)

The "electromagnetic radiation (EMR)" frequency spectrum is made up of a full range of frequencies and wavelengths of separate bands, such as: electricity, radiowaves, microwaves, infrared, visible light, ultraviolet, x-rays and gamma rays.

Each band is classified into the following radiation bands: Gamma; X-ray; Ultraviolet; Visible light; Infrared; Milliwave, Microwave; Radiowave; Shortwave; Mediumwave; Low-wave; and Electric and Magnetic fields. Below are the authorised terms for frequency bands commonly used in military communications and technical teaching of the past. Supplied by George Parker

EXTREMELY LOW FREQUENCY (ELF) (3-30Hz):

electric-magnetic fields (EFs-MFs)

EMF means "electric-magnetic fields" and "electromotive force"

RADIOFREQUENCY RADIATION (RFR) (30Hz-300GHz)

LOW WAVE (30Hz-300kHz):

Super Low (SLF), Ultra Low (ULF), Very Low (VLF), and Low Frequency (LF)

MEDIUM WAVE (300kHz-3MHz):

Medium Frequency (MF)

SHORT WAVE (3-30MHz):

High Frequency (HF)

RADIO WAVE (30-300MHz):

Very High Frequency (VHF)

MICRO WAVE (300MHz-30GHz):

Ultra-High Frequency (UHF) (300MHz-3GHz) and Super High Frequency (SHF) (3-30GHz)

MILLIMETER WAVE (30-300GHz):

Extra High Frequency (EHF)

| Designation | Frequencies |
|---|---|
| ELF (extremely low frequency) | 3-30 Hz |
| SLF (super low frequency) | 30–300 Hz |
| ULF (ultra low frequency) | 300–3000 Hz |
| VLF (very low frequency) | 3 – 30 kHz |
| LF (low frequency) | 30 kHz – 300 kHz |
| MF (medium frequency) | 300 kHz – 3 MHz |
| HF (high frequency) | 3 MHz – 30 MHz |
| VHF (very high frequency) | 30 MHz – 300 MHz |
| UHF (ultra high frequency) | 300 MHz – 3 GHz |
| SHF (super high frequency) | 3 GHz – 30 GHz |
| EHF (extremely high frequency) | 30 GHz – 300 GHz |

# Electromagnetic Radiation Spectrum

*Source: Saliev et al. 2018. "Biological effects of non-ionizing electromagnetic fields: Two sides of a coin."*

## ELECTROMAGNETIC AND RADIO WAVE SPECTRUM EXPLAINED

**THE ELECTROMAGNETIC SPECTRUM INCLUDES**: Direct Current (DC) (zero Hertz) - Alternating current (AC) in electrical circuits and electrical equipment, dirty electricity (built environment); AM Radio, FM Radio, TV, Mobile (Cell) phones, Wi-Fi, Satellite Technology, up to X-rays and Gama Rays known as ionizing radiation, with sufficient energy to damage DNA instantly.

The **RADIO WAVE SPECTRUM** sits inside the ELECTROMAGNETIC SPECTRUM. All radio waves and frequencies are different lengths depending on the frequency measured in hertz that travel at the speed of light. One Hertz is one wavelength, which is the distance from wave crest to wave crest and frequency is once cycle per second. Low frequency is a long wave and high frequency is a short wave, known as millimetre waves and microwaves.

## Hertz Frequencies and the Electromagnetic Spectrum

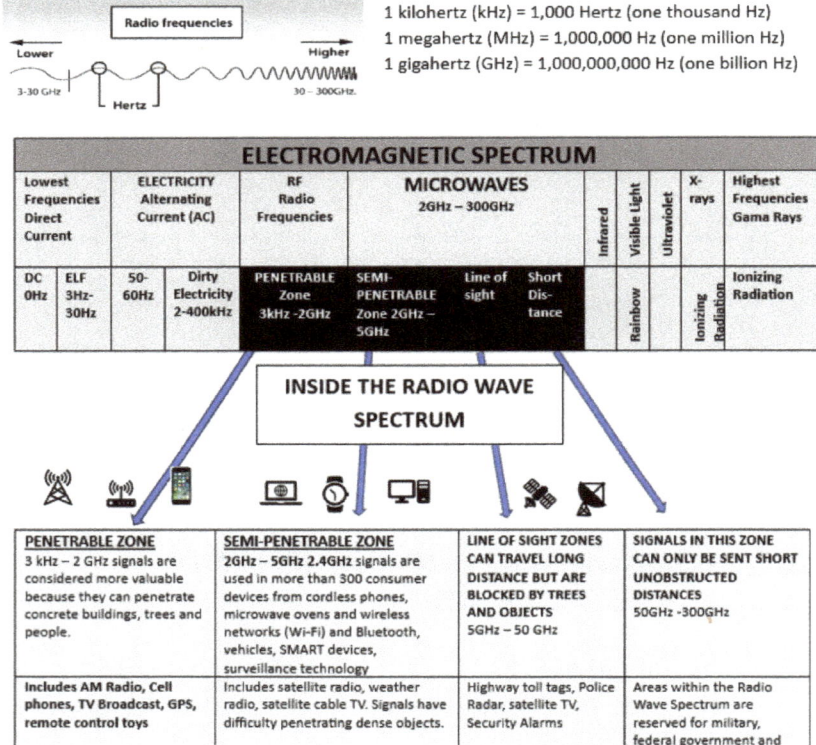

1 kilohertz (kHz) = 1,000 Hertz (one thousand Hz)
1 megahertz (MHz) = 1,000,000 Hz (one million Hz)
1 gigahertz (GHz) = 1,000,000,000 Hz (one billion Hz)

NOTE: SMART stand for "Self-Monitoring, Analysis, and Reporting Technology."

# WHAT IS A SAFE LEVEL OF RADIO-FREQUENCY RADATION

(High Frequency, Electromagnetic Waves are tested with a Radio-Frequency Analyser – RF meter)

**Evaluation Guidelines** for Sleeping areas according to the Building Biology Guidelines 2015:

**Power density** is calculated in microwatts per square meter: $\mu W/m^2$

**NO Anomaly = <0.1** $\mu W/m^2$

**Slight Anomaly = 0.1 – 10** $\mu W/m^2$

**Severe Anomaly = 10-100** $\mu W/m^2$

**Extreme Anomaly = >1000** $\mu W/m^2$

Values apply to single RF sources, e.g. GSM, UMTS, TETRA, LTE, WiMAX, Radio, TV, WLAN, DECT, Bluetooth …and refer to peak measurements. They do not apply to rotating-antenna radar.

More critical RF sources like pulsed or periodic signals (GSM, TETRA, DEC, WLAN, digital broadcasting …and broadband technologies with pulsed signals / pattens (UMTS, LTE) should be assessed more seriously, especially at higher levels and less critical RF sources like non-pulsed and non-periodic signals (FM, short, medium, long-wave, analogue broadcasting) should be assessed more generously, especially at low levels.

**ICNIRP allows up to 10,000,000 $\mu W/m^2$ - this is 10 million times more than the safe level suitable for sensitive people.**

# ENDNOTES

1   **International Appeal: Scientists call for Protection from Non-ionizing Electromagnetic Field Exposure** *https://emfscientist.org/index.php/ emf-scientist-appeal*

2   *Barrie Trower – "The Truth About 5G & Wi-Fi" – Part 1. https://rumble.com/ v2930dw-dr.-barrie-trower-the-truth-about-5g-and-wi-fi-part-1.html*

3   *Bandar. P and Carpenter. D. 2018. Planetary electromagnetic pollution: it is time to assess its impact. https://www.thelancet.com/journals/lanplh/article/ PIIS2542-5196(18)30221-3/fulltext*

4   *Vandana Shiva. Oneness vs the 1%. Spinifex Press,2018*

5   *IMDb: Plot summary of the Matrix movie: https://www.imdb.com/title/tt0133093/ plotsummary/*

6   *Patricia Burke's Substack for Safe Tech International patriciaburke@substack.com*

7   *Patricia Burke. Conspiracies; what you need to know https://naturalblaze. com/2021/02/timepeace-6-political-narratives-and-urgent-decision-making-covid-climate-censorship-and-domestic-terror.htm*

8   *Magda Havas, Canada. History of EMF. https://www.electrosensitivesociety.com/ history-of-the-illness/*

9   *Cook HJ, Steneck NH, Vander AJ, Kane GL. Early research on the biological effects of microwave radiation: 1940-1960. Ann Sci. 1980 May;37(3):323-51. doi: 10.1080/00033798000200271. PMID: 11610730. https://pubmed.ncbi.nlm.nih. gov/11610730/*

10  *Hecht (2016) Health implications of Long-term Exposure to Electrosmog. https:// manhattanneighbors.org/k-hecht/*

11  *EMF Wise, a website dedicated to Safe EMF: https://www.emfwise.com/*

12  *Australian Radiation Protection and Nuclear Safety Agency: https://www.arpansa. gov.au/understanding-radiation/radiation-sources/more-radiation-sources/ mobile-phones#cause*

13  *https://www.arpansa.gov.au/understanding-radiation/radiation-sources/ more-radiation-sources/mobile-phones#can-my-child-use-a-mobile-phone*

14    Environmental Health Trust (EHT): https://ehtrust.org/

15    EH Trust website, letters written to President Biden in 2021 and President Trump in 2019: https://ehtrust.org/dear-president-biden-halt-5g-assess-environmental-impact-minimize-technology-health-effects-to-children/

16    EH Trust wins court case: https://ehtrust.org/in-historic-decision-federal-court-finds-fcc-failed-to-explain-why-it-ignored-scientific-evidence-showing-harm-from-wireless-radiation/

17    EHT video presentation about the EHT vs FCC court case. Devra Davis presents history of cell phones and the reasons FCC standards are no longer relevant. https://www.youtube.com/watch?v=Qb42IZrMwFg

18

19    https://ehtrust.org/what-evidence-of-people-injured-by-wireless-radiation-was-ignored-by-the-fcc-historic-lawsuit-eht-et-al-v-fcc/

20    A Parliamentary Inquiry into 5G in Australia: https://www.aph.gov.au/Parliamentary_Business/Committees/House/Communications/5G

21    ICNIRP, International Commission on Non-Ionizing Radiation Protection: https://www.icnirp.org/en/about-icnirp/commission/index.html https://www.icnirp.org/en/about-icnirp/funding-governance/index.html

22    Barrie Trower PhD. Military microwave expert: YouTube link: Dr. Barrie Trower – "The Truth About 5G & Wi-Fi – Part 1.

23    https://www.wellintent.net/resources/Barrie-Trower-article-prepared-for King-of Botswana

24    Australian Parliamentary Inquiry 2018: Health & Aged Care and Biotoxin Illness: https://www.aph.gov.au/Parliamentary_Business/Committees/House/Health_Aged_Care_and_Sport/BiotoxinIllnesses/Report

25    Australian Parliamentary Inquiry 2019: Rollout of 5G in Australia https://www.aph.gov.au/Parliamentary_Business/Committees/House/Communications/5G

26    Surviving Mold: https://www.survivingmold.com/legal-resources/publications/papers-by-dr-ritchie-shoemaker

27    Shoemaker et all. 2010. Research Committee Report on Diagnosis and Treatment of Chronic Inflammatory Response Syndrome Caused by Exposure to the Interior Environment of Water-Damaged Buildings JULY 27, 2010. https://irp-cdn.multiscreensite.com/562d25c6/files/uploaded/Research%20Committee%20Report%20on%20Diagnosis%20and%20Treatment%20of%20CIRS%20WDB_July%2027_2010.pdf

28    Seletun Statement, Karalinska Institute, Press Statement: https://www.iemfa.org/seletun-statement/

29    The BioInitiative Report 2012. A Rationale for Biologically-based Exposure Standards for Low-Intensity Electromagnetic Radiation: https://bioinitiative.org/table-of-contents/

30   *Australian Medical Association, Oath: https://www.ama.com.au/media/ ama-adopts-wma-declaration-geneva*

31   *Dr Charlie Teo. TV interview on mobile phone and brain cancer risk_60 Minutes: https://www.youtube.com/watch?v=mMKwtjO73Y8*

32   *ECSFR Letter to Dr Brendan Murphy Legal Notice; Cease and Desist – Safety of 5G Technology. www.wellintent.net.essential-reading*

33   *ES-UK.info. Social Exclusion to Electromagnetic Pollution: A Belgian Perspective. Go to: Electric Sensitivity UK: http://www.es-uk.info/*

34   *ES-UK.info: https://www.es-uk.info/resources/*

35   *MCH and EHS are Linked: Belpomme D, Irigaray P. Why electrohypersensitivity and related symptoms are caused by non-ionizing man-made electromagnetic fields: An overview and medical assessment. Environ Res. 2022 Sep;212(Pt A):113374. doi: 10.1016/j.envres.2022.113374. Epub 2022 May 7. PMID: 35537497. https:// pubmed.ncbi.nlm.nih.gov/35537497/*

36   *The Truth About Cancer Series: https://thetruthaboutcancer.com/*

37   *G. Edward Griffin. 2010.The Creature from Jekyll Island; A Second Look at the Federal Reserve: https://realityzone.com/*

38   *The Seletun Scientific Statement: Lower EMF Standards for World Health A re Urgently Needed, International Scientists Say. https://www.iemfa.org/seletun-statement/*

39   *Building Biology Institute: https://buildingbiology.com/about/*

40   *What to know about X-rays: https://www.medicalnewstoday.com/articles/219970*

41   *Arthur Firstenberg. The Invisible Rainbow: A History of Electricity and Life. 2017. AGB Press*

42   *Aurthur Firstenberg: https://cellphonetaskforce.org/wp-content/uploads/2023/11/ CURRICULUM-VITAE-of-Arthur-Firstenberg.pdf*

43   *Dr Bruce Lipton: Biology of Belief: Unleashing the Power of Consciousness, Matter, & Miracles https://www.brucelipton.com/*

44   *The Cell Phone and the Cell – the Role of Calcium, by Andrew Goldsworthy: https://www.radiationresearch.org/research/ the-cell-phone-and-the-cell-the-role-of-calcium-by-dr-andrew-goldsworthy/*

45   *5G: Great risk for EU, U.S. and International Health! Compelling Evidence for Eight Distinct Types of Great Harm Caused by Electromagnetic Field (EMF) Exposures and the Mechanism that Causes Them: https://www.fcc.gov/ecfs/ document/10910251807127/1*

46   *Dr. Bruce Lipton; The Wisdom of Your Cells. https://www.brucelipton.com/store/ all-products/*

47   *Frederic W. Miller MD on The Increasing Prevalence of Autoimmunity and Autoimmune Diseases: An Urgent Call to Action for Improved Understanding, Diagnosis, Treatment and Prevention. https://pmc.ncbi.nlm.nih.gov/articles/PMC9918670/*

48  Samuel Milham MD. MPH. Dirty Electricity; Electrification and the Diseases of Civilization. 2012 Second Edition. iUniverse

49  5G – An Undeniable Risk Webinar. Includes Dr. Paul Heroux, Dr. Kent Chamberlin, Dr. Sharon Goldberg, Frank Clegg and Andrew Campanelli, Esq. https://www.youtube.com/watch?v=_ltJdtmsAS8

50  Dr Sharon Goldberg: YouTube presentation to Congress October 2018; Presentation to Congress to testimony in opposition to Senate Bill 637 and 894, pertaining to 5G wireless infrastructure legislation, which passed through the Michigan House Energy Policy Committee with a vote 15 to 4. https://www.youtube.com/watch?v=WiVE6RE-3Ic

51  David Icke on Problem – Reaction – Solution: https://davidicke.com/2022/05/18/problem-reaction-solution-david-icke-talking-in-2010/

52  Architects and Engineer for 9/11 Truth: https://www.ae911truth.org/

53  Know Your Rights Group. Australia: Port Arthur Massacre. https://www.knowyourrightsgroup.com.au/conspiracy/

54  Cairns News, Port Arthur Massacre: Cairns News, Port Arthur Massacre: https://cairnsnews.org/category/port-arthur/

55  Environmental Working Group, Asbestos Facts: https://www.epa.gov/asbestos

56  Author William (Bill) Cooper, Behold a Pale Horse. USA Navy Intelligence insider, exposed the covert operations of the CIA, and US Government political collusion.

57  Charlene Acres, Ottawa; daughter struggles to attend school due to EHS https://www.youtube.com/watch?v=A6yUpx9Ved8

58  Nick Pineault, The EMF Guy, Canada. Interview with Maria August, about EHS and the difficulties living in the modern world. Maria took her own life. https://www.youtube.com/watch?v=1dEZisLvruU&t=2s

59  Electrosensitivity: Tortured by Technology? BBC Stories, Short Documentary: https://www.youtube.com/watch?v=MBNTVjNS5VE

60  Dr. Magda Havas, PhD. https://magdahavas.com/

61  Dr. Magda Havas, PhD. On Electrohypersensitivity: https://www.youtube.com/watch?v=VeURQ9Hc3jA

62  ES-UK.info: https://www.es-uk.info/resources/

63  Electromagnetic Sensitivity and Electromagnetic Hypersensitivity, (also known as Asthenic Sickness, EMF Intolerance Sickness, Idiopathic Environmental Intolerance – EMF. Microwave syndrome, Radio Wave Sickness) A Summary by Michael Bevington (Capability Books UK). 2010: https://www.es-uk.info/electromagnetic-sensitivity-and-electromagnetic-hypersensitivity/

64  Environmental Medical Centre, Richardson, Dallas, Texas: https://www.ehcd.com/welcome-to-the-environmental-health-center-dallas

65  What is the impact of electromagnetic waves on epileptic seizures? https://pubmed.ncbi.nlm.nih.gov/23676765/

66   Lauraine Vivian and Olle Johansson. ACADEMIA Letters Technological Singularity: Knowledge Translation and Ethics: https://www.researchgate.net/publication/353484144_ACADEMIA_Letters_Technological_Singularity_Knowledge_Translation_and_Ethics

67   Bruce Lipton. PhD. Spontaneous Evolution: Our positive future and a way to get from there to here. 2012 Hay House Publishing. https://www.brucelipton.com/product/spontaneous-evolution/

68   Null et al. 2022 Death by Medicine: https://canadahealthalliance.org/death-by-medicine/

69   Dr Samuel H. Epstein: The Politics of Cancer Revisited. 1998 East Ridge Press. USA https://openlibrary.org/books/OL378995M/The_politics_of_cancer_revisited

70   Stockholm Convention on Persistent Organic Pollutants: https://pops.int/TheConvention/Overview/tabid/3351/Default.aspx

71   International Agency for Research on Cancer: https://www.iarc.who.int/

72   Healthy Building Network (HBN) Report. Joe Thornton PhD. Environmental Impacts of Polyvinyl Chloride (PVC) building materials: https://habitablefuture.org/wp-content/uploads/2024/03/94-environmental-impacts-of-polyvinyl-chloride-building-materials.pdf

73   Fluoride Action Network: https://fluoridealert.org/

74   Dr Stephanie Seneff PDF of presentation on Glyphosate: https://people.csail.mit.edu/seneff/2018/Toronto_vaccines.pdf

75   Children's Health Defence on Glyphosate: https://childrenshealthdefense.org/known-culprits/glyphosate/

76   Vaccine documentary: 1986: The Act 2020. https://www.imdb.com/video/vi4058890777/?playlistId=tt12708236&ref_=tt_ov_ov_vi

77   VAXXED; From Coverup to Catastrophe, documentary: https://www.imdb.com/title/tt5562652/?ref_=tt_mlt_i_1

78   Environmental Working Group: Environmental Working Group: https://www.ewg.org/

79   Dr Richie Shoemaker. Surviving Mold: https://www.survivingmold.com/resources-for-patients/diagnosis

80   Dr Richie Shoemaker, Surviving Mold: https://www.survivingmold.com/about/ritchie-shoemaker-m-d

81   Goldberg, K. Founder of Electroplague: Dr Dietrich Klinghardt reveals what happens to mould when exposed to wireless radiation: https://electroplague.com/2013/06/03/video-mold-toxins-skyrocket-with-emr-exposure/

82   Nanowerk, SMART Tech and the Internet of Things (IoT): https://www.nanowerk.com/smart/internet-of-things-explained.php

83   AI-generated personas and deepfake videos: https://www.gendigital.com/blog/news

84  INTERNET OF BIO-NANO THINGS: A REVIEW OF APPLICATIONS, ENABLING TECHNOLOGIES AND KEY CHALLENGES. https://www.itu.int/dms_pub/itu-s/opb/jnl/S-JNL-VOL2.ISSUE3-2021-A08-PDF-E.pdf

85  IoBNT by Sabrina on Odysee: https://odysee.com/@BKBlair:e/David_Icke_in_the_Hive_and_routing_the_IoBnT_1%E2%A7%B82_a7f1fcec5da4b7:9

86  John Stauber and Sheldon Rampton. Toxic Sludge is Good For You! Lies, Damn Lies and the Public Relations Industry. 2002.  https://www.amazon.com/Toxic-Sludge-Good-You-Relations/dp/1567510604

87  G. Edward Griffin. The Creature From Jekyll Island: A Second Look at the Federal Reserve. 5th Edition. 2010. American Media.

88  EMR Shielding material available from Safe Living Technologies Canada: https://safelivingtechnologies.com/

89  EMR Shielding material available from Safer EMF in Australia: https://www.saferemf.com.au/ or

90  Shielding material available from EMR Australia or Gigahertz Solutions Germany: https://emraustralia.com.au/ or https://gigahertz-solutions.com/Shielding/Fabrics

91  Mobile phone radiation reduction covers:
    Mobile Safety Australia https://mobilesafety.com.au/
    Vest Tech USA https://vesttech.com/

92  Blocking nocturnal blue light for insomnia: https://cdn.shopify.com/s/files/1/1014/4865/files/Blocking_nocturnal_blue_light_for_insomnia_A_randomized_controlled_trial.pdf?v=1618809507

93  Block Blue Light Glasses: https://www.blockbluelight.com.au/pages/about-us

94  Blue Light Filters for Screens: https://www.geckoandfly.com/21437/blue-light-filter/

95  Clint Ober: Earthing; The Most Important Health Discovery Ever! 2010. Basic Health Publication, INC

96  Clint Ober website: https://www.earthing.com/pages/what-is-grounding

97  Dawson Church. The Astonishing Science of How Your Brain Creates Material Reality. 2018. Hay House Inc.

98  Dawson Church. Emotion Freedom Techniques. 2017. Hay House Inc.

99  Dr Joe Dispenza. You are the Placebo; Making Your Mind Matter. 2014. Hay House Inc

100 Dr Joe Dispenza. Becoming Supernatural; How Common People Are Doing the Uncommon. 2017. Hay House Inc.

101 Chris Woollams. Everything You Need to Know to Help You Beat Cancer. 2005. Health Issues Limited

102 Chris Woollams. The Rainbow Diet and how it can help you beat cancer. 2010. Health Issues Limited

103 Bill Statham. The Chemical Maze Shopping Companion. 2006. Summerdale Self Help.

104 *Environmental Working Group: Products search: https://www.ewg.org/ ewgverified/products.php?models=cosmetic%2Cdiaper&search=&minority_ owned=&brand=&category=&sort=newest&type=*

105 *Dr Stephanie Seneff eposes the truth about Glyphosate: YouTube https://www.youtube. com/watch?v=Z8xuyoKZv4s*

106 *Dr Stephanie Seneff with Dr Andrew Wong from Capital Integrative Health (CIH) https://www.youtube.com/watch?v=f5Xjj3t96fI*

107 *Learn more about dowsing with Raymon Grace at: https://www.raymongrace.us/ about-dowsing.html#/*

108 *Gerald H. Pollack. The Fourth Phase of Water: Beyond solid, liquid and vapor. 2013 Ebner & Sons.*

109 *Dr. Masaru Emoto website: https://masaru-emoto.net/en/*

110 *The story and history surrounding the life of Royal Raymond Rife, and his Rife Ray Tube system to treat cancer. https://www.royal-rife-machine.com/Royal-Rife.htm*

111 *Cancer predictions according to WHO and IARC: https://www.who.int/news/ item/01-02-2024-global-cancer-burden-growing--amidst-mounting-need-for-services*

112 *Age of Aquarius: https://astrologystargazing.com/ when-is-the-age-of-aquarius-understanding-its-timing-and-significance/*

113 *Age of Aquarius, what it means for our world: https://www.astrolis.com/astrology/ age-of-aquarius*

114 *Mahzarin Banaji and Anthony Greenwald. Blind Spot; Hidden Biases of Good People. 2013. Random House*

115 *Matt Gawitch PhD; Biases Are Neither All Good Nor All Bad: https:// www.psychologytoday.com/intl/blog/hovercraft-full-eels/202009/ biases-are-neither-all-good-nor-all-bad*

116 *Robert Cialdinit. Influence: The psychology of persuasion. 2007. Collins. New York*

117 *Learned Helplessness: Seligman's Theory of Depression. https://positivepsychology.com/ learned-helplessness-seligman-theory-depression-cure/*

118 *Lauren Slater. Opening Skinner's box: great psychological experiments of the 20th century. 2005. W.W. Norton. New York*

119 *Australia One Party: an alternative to regular political parties https://www. australiaoneparty.com/*

120 *Children's Health Defence: The Fight Against Monsanto's Roundup: https:// live.childrenshealthdefense.org/chd-tv/shows/good-morning-chd-2023/ the-fight-against-monsantos-roundup/*

121 *Stephanie Senneff PhD. TOXIC LEGACY; How the Weedkiller GLYSOPHATE is Destroying Our Health and the Environment. 2021 Chelsea Green Publishing.*

122 *Robert F. Kennedy Jr., interview on YouTube about glyphosate (Roundup). https://www. youtube.com/watch?v=-dwWQZkJ5r8*

123 Bruce Lipton. PhD. Biology of Belief; Unleashing the Power of Consciousness, Matter, & Miracles. 2016 Hay House Inc.

124 John Diamond M.D. Your Body Doesn't Lie; Unlock the power of your natural energy! 1979 Mass Market Paperback.

125 Dr. Peter Dingle. Medical Myths & Health Lies That Are Killing Us. 2014. Barker Dean Publishing. Australia

126 Economic Times: How a Nobel-nominated scientist was cancelled for exposing the invisible danger we face every day: https://economictimes.indiatimes.com/magazines/panache/how-a-nobel-prize-nominated-scientist-was-cancelled-for-exposing-the-invisible-danger-of-electromagnetic-frequencies-we-face-every-day/articleshow/120879161.cms

127 Wikipedia explanation of a paradigm: https://en.wikipedia.org/wiki/Paradigm

128 Stephen R. Covey. The 7 Habits of Highly Effective People: Restoring the Character Ethic. [Rev. ed.]. New York: Free Press, 2004.

129 Dan Buettner: The Blue Zones: Lessons for Living Longer From the People Who've Lived the Longest. Washington, D.C., National Geographic, 2008.

130 Dementia Australia: https://www.dementia.org.au/about-dementia/dementia-facts-and-figures

131 Climate Viewer News. Where Conspiracy Meets Reality. https://climateviewer.com/

132 North American Indigenous Principle for Sustainability: https://www.ictinc.ca/blog/seventh-generation-principle

133 Building Biology Institute, 25 Guiding Principles: https://buildingbiologyinstitute.org/about/25-principles-of-building-biology/

134 Wellintent & Building Biology Resources: https://wellintent.net/resources

135 Keith Cutter. Do Harmonizers Work? https://keithcutter.substack.com/p/emf-harmonizers-neutralizers-blockers.

136 Oceania Radiofrequency Scientific Advisory Association, article on Harmonizers; do they work? https://www.orsaa.org/product-disclaimer.html

137 Military + Aerospace Electronics website: https://www.militaryaerospace.com/communications/article/16707029/shortwave-infrared-laser-detection-and-tracking-on-the-battlefield

138 International Tribunal for Natural Justice https://commission.itnj.org/

139 International Tribunal for Natural Justice. Weaponisation of the Biosphere https://commission.itnj.org/weaponisation-biosphere/

140 Event 201 – John Hopkins University – Preparation for a world wide pandemic, event: https://centerforhealthsecurity.org/our-work/tabletop-exercises/event-201-pandemic-tabletop-exercise

141 Dr Thomas Cowan, The Contagion Myth; Why Viruses (including "Coronavirus") Are Not the Cause of Disease. https://drtomcowan.com/products/the-contagion-myth/

142   Sayer Ji, Substack. *Four years of Lawfare and Black Ops:* https://sayerji.substack.com/p/four-years-of-lawfare-and-black-ops

143   Sayer Ji Substack interview, how they shut him down, for telling the truth: https://sayerji.substack.com/p/silenced-for-telling-the-truth-about?publication_id=2878303&post_id=163397168&isFreemail=true&r=8lllt&triedRedirect=true

144   *Truth About Cancer article (compliments of James Corbett) exposing the Disinformation Dozen:* https://thetruthaboutvaccines.com/real-disinformation-dozen/

145   James Corbett, *The Corbett Report: 5th Generation Warfare:* https://corbettreport.com/your-guide-to-fifth-generation-warfare/

146   Mountain Quest Retreat; Wi-Fi free zone; https://www.mountainquestretreats.com/

147   Radiation Refuge: https://www.radiationrefuge.com/myrrhee-victoria-refuge

148   Robyn Williams, *In Love With Betty the Crow. The first 40 years of ABC RN's The Science Show.* 2016. Harper Collins, Australia.

149   Elizabeth Blackburn https://en.wikipedia.org/wiki/Elizabeth_Blackburn

150   Stop World Control, a website by David Sorensen, to help wake up the world: https://stopworldcontrol.com/

151   Keith Cutter, EMF Testing Technician. YouTube: https://www.youtube.com/@emfremedy.

152   Keith Cutter, EMF Remedy: Substack  https://keithcutter.substack.com/p/emf-challenge-facilities-a-vision

153   Dr William Rae. Keynote address: Building Biology Conference 2011. https://www.youtube.com/watch?v=_b5cUfBVIJw

154   Ty Bollinger. *Monumental Myths of the Modern Medical Mafia and the Mainstream Media and the Multitude of Lying Liars That Manufactured Them.* 2013. Infinity 510² Partners. USA